"Noel Yeatts's life will awaken yours. Her personal witness to stories of triumph and tragedy will inspire Christians to get out of the pew and into the world."

Gabe Lyons, author of *The Next Christians*
and founder of Q Ideas

"Noel saw a need and was willing to feel it and has written about it in this fabulous book. She realizes that it only takes one to reach one, and in this book you will find her story and others that can encourage you to make a difference to someone's quality of liferight now. She also encourages you to find your passion and use it to launch the wellspring of generosity that is in your heart. Go see the need and help fill it. Everyone needs hope, and this is a book of hope for the hopeless, help for the helpless, and healing for those in despair. I've seen firsthand the work that Noel is doing. She isn't a woman just 'talking'—she walks the walk!"

Thelma Wells, author, speaker, teacher, A Woman
of God Ministries; www.ThelmaWells.com

"Noel Brewer Yeatts is a global leader. Her work in the world's most difficult places is changing history right now, and after you read *Awake*, you'll understand why. This isn't just a book. It's a provocation. By the time you're finished, you'll be making history too."

Johnnie Moore, vice president, Liberty University;
author of *Honestly: Really Living What We Say We Believe*

"Sometimes the world's problems feel too big, and we're overwhelmed into apathy. In moments like that you need a clear prophetic voice to wake you from complacency, bringing clarity and focus. Noel is one such voice, speaking with every fiber of her life. She calls us from our preoccupied lives to see the world beyond our shores. It's uncomfortable and challenging, but Noel is not trying to guilt us into action. Her stories remind us that the world is changed by everyday people like us. This book remind us of what is possible for those who dare."

Jo Saxton, 3 Dimension Ministries; speaker and author

"Noel Yeatts is a powerful voice for the forgotten. When God hears the cries of his children, he looks for a deliverer, and the deliverer he calls is you and me. The destiny of thousands is directly linked to our obedience and our willingness to take a risk so that others might live. *Awake* challenges us to take our eyes off self and to pursue the life we were chosen to live."

Danita Estrella, founder/CEO of Danita's Children and Hope for Haiti Children's Center

"The heart cannot taste what the eyes have not seen. In *Awake*, Noel powerfully communicates her extraordinary encounters with extreme need and profound opportunity from all across the globe. As a result, this is a book from the heart and for every heart that truly wants to make a difference in today's world."

Daniel Henderson, author of *Transforming Prayer*

"Noel Brewer Yeatts is doing as much to ease the pain and heartache in our world today as anyone else I know. This book, *Awake*, is a wake-up call for the rest of us to step up and help make a difference. I encourage you to read this book and then make the commitment that you, like Noel, will be fully engaged in reaching out to help those in need. Please read this book today."

Jonathan Falwell, pastor of Thomas Road Baptist Church

AWAKE

Doing a WORLD of Good One Person at a Time

Noel Brewer Yeatts

BakerBooks
a division of Baker Publishing Group
Grand Rapids, Michigan

Published by Baker Books
a division of Baker Publishing Group
P.O. Box 6287, Grand Rapids, MI 49516-6287
www.bakerbooks.com

Printed in the United States of America

Library of Congress Cataloging-in-Publication Data
Yeats, Noel Brewer, 1972–
    Awake : doing a world of good one person at a time / Noel Brewer Yeatts.
        p. cm.
    Includes bibliographical references (p.   ).
    ISBN 978-0-8010-1458-1 (pbk.)
    1. Church work with the poor. 2. Distributive justice—Religious aspects—Christianity. 3. Christian stewardship. 4. Yeatts, Noel Brewer, 1972– I. Title.
    BV639.P6Y43 2012
    261.8′325—dc22   2012000776

All dates, place names, titles, and events in this account are factual. The names of certain characters have been changed in order to protect their privacy.

The author has made every effort to provide the most up-to-date statistics in this book; however, many statistics are constantly changing.

Published in association with literary agent David Van Diest of D. C. Jacobson and Associates, www.dcjacobson.com, 3689 Carman Drive, Suite 300, Lake Oswego, OR 97035.

12 13 14 15 16 17 18   7 6 5 4 3 2 1

Contents

For Nildo—
my life would never be the same after meeting you . . .
and for that, I am forever grateful.

Introduction

You were born in the developed world. You have parents and a family. You have a place to live and call home. You have an education and endless opportunities. You have food, clothing, and access to healthcare. Okay, maybe you don't have everything you want, but if you are honest, you do have everything you need. Lucky you . . .

But let's burst that bubble you are living in for just a moment. Over one billion people in the world don't live like you do. And as Bono says, "Where you live should no longer determine *whether* you live!"[1]

If you simply have some food in your fridge, a place to sleep, and some clothes to wear, you are already better off than 75 percent of the world.

Just drinking the water out of the faucet in your kitchen makes you better off than 1.5 billion people.

Having just a little bit of money makes you part of the top 8 percent of the world's wealthy.

While more than 3 million people around the world cannot freely attend religious or political events without fear of some kind of punishment or retaliation, you are free to do as you wish.

And just the fact that you picked up this book and are reading it makes you luckier than 2 billion people who simply cannot read.[2]

Are you beginning to wake up?

I wouldn't call this a problem—it is an all-out crisis of epic proportion. But what are we really doing about it?

Timothy Keller says, "Many people who are evidently genuine Christians do not demonstrate much concern for the poor. How do we account for that? I would like to believe that a heart for the poor 'sleeps' down in a Christian's soul until it is awakened. . . . I believe, however, when justice for the poor is connected not to guilt but to grace and to the gospel, this 'pushes the button' down deep in believers' souls, and they begin to wake up."[3]

One of my favorite magazines is no longer in publication. It was called *Need*, and it focused on humanitarian efforts around the world. Its motto was this: "We are not out to save the world but to tell the stories of those who are."

In some ways, that is how I feel about this book. Yes, you will see my story intertwined with others in the following pages, but my story is nothing more than the story of those who have touched my life, broken my heart, and restored my hope in humanity, justice, and God's love.

Ultimately this is a story about change: the change that can take place both in your life and in the lives of people around the world once we are truly awake. I hope that you will find at least part of your life story in the lives of the poor and disenfranchised of our world.

May we all find ourselves awake and doing a world of good.

1

The Lucky One

Save one life. Save the world.
Talmud (Book of Jewish Law)[1]

I left Virginia in February bundled up for winter and landed in Guatemala where it was over 100 degrees. The heat was absolutely stifling.

It didn't help that I was in a village with no shade, no trees, no buildings to go into—just a big dusty field. Floodwaters and mudslides had completely destroyed the village months earlier, leaving the people homeless. They had lost everything. The government relocated them but did little more than give them a piece of barren land. Makeshift shelters filled the village. Garbage bags held up by sticks were the housing of choice. Dilapidated shacks lined the dusty roads. Since the village had no electricity, no sewage system, and no access to clean water, disease and illness ran rampant there.

The recent storm that destroyed their village was the latest problem the people faced. Their other struggles went back as long as they could remember.

I've been told that 60 percent of Guatemalans drink contaminated water. Two-thirds of children live in poverty,[2] while 43 percent of children under five suffer from chronic malnutrition.[3] Guatemala suffers in severe need.

I helped our team distribute packs of food—rice, beans, oil, and other staples to last a family for one month. Villagers lined up in the hot sun, eager to get their own bags. They knew that without the packages, feeding their families would be nearly impossible.

After the food distribution, I rode to the other side of the village to see some new homes that were under construction. It was only a couple, but that was true progress in a place with so little.

A truck carrying a big tank filled with water drove by. The driver went door to door selling buckets of water for about six *quetzales* a liter—the equivalent of about one dollar. That doesn't sound like much, but it's more than the average person there makes in a week, so it is a huge expense. Unfortunately, the water from the truck was contaminated. People used what little money they had to buy water that would most likely make them sick.

More than 2,500 people lived in this village, each one of them struggling to survive.

Everywhere I looked, I saw a need—the people needed homes, food, water, health care, a school—they needed everything! Their needs were not luxuries; they were necessities. It was a matter of life and death.

It was overwhelming.

A young girl and her mother walked toward me. I recognized them from earlier, when they'd been standing in line to receive food. I soon could tell that they were heading directly to me.

I am still not sure why they chose me, especially when so many other Americans were standing around that day, but they walked right up to me. I knew immediately that something was terribly wrong. With a look of desperation, the mother was clenching a plastic bag of papers.

Shy, the little girl clung to her mother's side, obviously scared. She was beautiful. Her long, dark hair was pulled back in a ponytail, and she wore a green skirt and orange top. She was nine years old, and her name was Margarita.

I wondered what they needed. Not all stories in life are pretty. Some, I would rather not hear—especially when the story involves a child. My heart can barely take it. I was afraid this might be one of those stories, but I was drawn to this little girl, and she was drawn to me.

He was only one among millions. Easily forgotten and too small to be noticed, he was just five years old.

He lived his days on the streets of one of the roughest cities in the world. His home was a cardboard box; he walked with no shoes, wore little clothing, and begged for any food he could get.

Every day was the same. He had one purpose—survival. Abandoned by his father and ignored by his mother, he had a slim chance of making it on the streets.

Hundreds of thousands of people passed by him every single day. Maybe they didn't notice the little boy wearing nothing but dirty underwear as he slept on a public bench. Maybe they didn't care.

At the time, Brazil was a country with millions of street children—some analysts estimate as many as seven million![4] No one could solve the massive problem, so people quit noticing, quit trying. They simply coexisted with these children they saw on the streets every day. "The problem with street children became so bad in the late 1980s that Brazil had 'large-scale, deliberate, systematic killing of street children by death squads who enjoyed a high degree of impunity for their actions.' . . .

'Street execution' was once listed by Amnesty International as the third leading cause of death for Brazilian children."[5]

These streets were Nildo's home.

No one showed concern for his deformed, shoeless feet. No one wondered what a wide-eyed five-year-old was doing wandering around alone. This helpless child was afraid and hungry with no one to protect him, no one to care for him. But Nildo captured my heart.

> "I think the purpose of life is to be useful, to be responsible, to be honorable, to be compassionate. It is, after all, to matter: to count, to stand for something, to have made some difference that you lived at all."
>
> Leo C. Rosten[6]

I was fifteen years old when I met him. I traveled to Rio de Janeiro, Brazil, with my family. My dad is the founder and president of World Help, but at that time he was working at a Christian university. On this particular trip he led a large group of college students to work in children's homes and present concerts in public schools, churches, and outdoor plazas. We were told that more than 500,000 people traveled by boat every day to and from work across the bay from Rio. We got permission to set up our sound equipment and instruments on the back of a flatbed trailer and park it next to the boat docks. Every thirty minutes, twenty or more large ferries carrying more than 5,000 people pulled into the docks.

As the crowds made their way home from work, we blasted the sound as loud as it would go and performed music in Portuguese. At the end of each concert, my dad gave a short message. The entire concert and presentation lasted around 45 minutes. We took a short break and then, as more boats began to arrive, we started all over again.

During one of those concerts, my sister and I wandered through the crowd that gathered. And that was when it happened. That was when we first saw Nildo.

The first thing we noticed was his clothes, or lack thereof. He had no shoes, no shirt, and no pants; he wore a pair of torn underwear. Through an interpreter, we found out that Nildo's father had abandoned him and his mother couldn't afford to take care of him. Nildo was a street child, left to fend for himself. He had no one.

Yet this little boy who had so little was full of personality. He warmed up to us right away, and even though we did not speak the same language, we made an instant connection.

I quickly looked for my dad. I had to tell him about this little boy. My sister said, "Dad, do you see that bench over there? That's where he sleeps, and he takes a shower underneath that drain pipe." I asked, "Do you think we could buy him some food and clothes?" My dad sent us off with little Nildo and one of our missionary friends, Donna, to go shopping.

We went to a nearby mall to get some lunch and clothes. We bought Nildo a Happy Meal at McDonald's. He devoured the food.

I still smile when I think about the bright yellow jogging suit he picked out and the new Nike shoes, so popular in the 1980s. We took him to the bathroom to clean him up a little before dressing him in his new clothes. As I washed his feet, I couldn't help but notice they were deformed, apparently from roaming the streets barefoot all of his life. When I slipped on his new Nikes, he kept saying "shoes" over and over in Portuguese—*sapatos, sapatos, sapatos*—as he pointed to his feet. He had never owned a pair of new shoes!

We brought Nildo back to the street where we had found him, and he didn't leave our side the whole afternoon. We never really thought about what we would do at the end of the day or where Nildo would go. We just enjoyed the moment, so happy to help him. He enjoyed all the attention.

When it started to get dark, the police rushed us to move the trailer and bus that our group performed on. Our vehicle blocked traffic, and everyone started yelling, so we packed up and left quickly.

It all happened so fast. I didn't have time to think about what to do with Nildo, but we knew we couldn't take him with us. As we got on the bus to leave, I looked out the window and saw him in his bright yellow clothes, waving good-bye. My heart broke for him.

By this time, the entire group knew Nildo, and we had all grown attached. Everyone on the bus cried at leaving him. One of the university students sitting in the back of our bus had been orphaned in Japan and raised by American parents. Watching as little Nildo waved while we drove away, he was overcome with emotion. For a few moments, no one spoke a word as his unrestrained sobbing carried to the front of the bus.

On our way back to the hotel, my sister and I launched a plan. We pleaded with my dad to do something to help Nildo. It just was not right. We couldn't leave him on the streets.

My dad made some phone calls and found a children's home close by that was willing to take him in. The cost was only about $400 for an entire year.

When we arrived at the hotel, my dad called all the students together and described what we could do for Nildo. He took off his hat and passed it around. It was the end of the trip, and all anyone had left was a little money for snacks and souvenirs. Raising $400 did not seem likely.

As we passed the hat, one of the Brazilian pastors who was helping us leaned over and said, "Why are you doing so much for this one child? Do you know how many orphaned children there are? There are thousands and thousands of homeless children on the streets of Brazil. There is no way you can help them all."

No way you can help them all—those words have played over and over in my head for years. To me, they were fighting words. A challenge. A dare that made me want to say, "Don't tell me what I can't do. Don't tell me I can't make a difference. Don't tell me I can't change the world."

Time and maturity have made me look differently at these words. Maybe the pastor was right. Perhaps one person can't save all the children in the world. But that was not what we were trying to do.

After the hat made its way around the group, we counted the money. There was more than $800—enough to provide two years of care for Nildo!

Excited, we returned to find Nildo the next day. As soon as we arrived, my sister and I frantically looked for him to give him the wonderful news, but we couldn't find him anywhere. We searched and searched where we'd found him the day before. Finally, after nearly an hour, we found him several blocks away, but we were not prepared for what we would find. The older street children had beat him up, taking his clothes and new shoes. All he had left was his dirty pair of torn underwear.

> "By compassion we make others' misery our own, and so, by relieving them, we relieve ourselves also."
>
> Thomas Browne, Sr.[7]

I will never forget the feeling of absolute horror and despair, knowing what Nildo experienced the night before. We held that broken little boy in our arms and vowed that he would not spend another day on the streets.

We brought Nildo back to the docks, and everyone crowded around to comfort him. My sister asked, "Dad, can we buy him some more new clothes?" He immediately said, "Yes, just don't get bright yellow this time." So off we went and returned with another jogging suit—gray—with an identical pair of Nike shoes.

We knew it would take more than new clothes to make a real difference in Nildo's life. We asked him if he wanted to get off the streets and live in a children's home where he would receive the love and care he needed. Of course, he said yes.

That night, as we prepared to leave, Nildo sat on the bus with us! When we arrived at the hotel, he needed to take a shower and get cleaned up, but he refused to take off his new shoes. Dad tried for thirty minutes to explain that he only had to take them off for five minutes while he was in the shower and then he could put them back on. Nildo didn't buy it. Finally, Dad made a deal with him: we would put his shoes where he could see them while he showered. This worked, and as soon as he was done and dried off, he put the shoes right back on. He even slept in them.

For the next year, we thought about Nildo often. We kept in touch and received reports that he was doing well in school, was attending church, and had even become a Christ follower. The following summer, my dad took another group of students back to Brazil. This time we could not join him, but we made him promise to visit Nildo and give him a picture of our family—and buy him some new shoes.

When my dad arrived in Brazil, he gave Nildo a Bible that all of us had signed and a framed photo of our family. He said that Nildo hugged and kissed the photo and told everyone around him in loud Portuguese, "These are my American sisters! They took me off the streets."

Later, my dad told us, "Girls, if you never do another good deed in your life, you have done something incredible for this one little boy."

Twenty years later and a world away, I stand in front of a few thousand women at a conference. It is early on a Saturday morning. The audience wakes up slowly, and I could really use another cup of coffee.

I tell the story of Nildo. I try to talk as animatedly as I can, hoping to hold the attention of at least a couple of people. A few minutes into the story, I am amazed. I have the crowd in the palm of my hand. They ooh and ahh at the photos of Nildo I show on the screens. One photo shows him the day we met, when he wore his torn underpants. His feet are bare. He is so cute, and everyone gets a good laugh at my 1980s big hair. (If you lived through that era, you know what I mean. And if you didn't—be glad!)

They see another photo of Nildo, all cleaned up in his new clothes, laughing and happy. And then they see my favorite photo—one of him and me together from just a few years ago when he came to visit in the States.

As I wrap up the story and tell what Nildo is doing today, I notice how quiet the room has become. Every time I tell his story, the reaction is the same. People listen intently, some tear up, and even years later if I see them again, they remember the story of the little boy in Brazil . . . our Nildo.

The Blind Side, based on a true story and starring Sandra Bullock, is a feel-good movie if there ever was one. Sandra's character, Leigh Anne Tuohy, rescued a virtually homeless boy, Michael Oher, off the streets of Memphis and brought him into her home with her husband and two children.

> "I know that God will not give me anything I can't handle. I just wish that he didn't trust me so much."
>
> Mother Teresa[8]

After a couple hours of twists and turns in the story, the movie reveals how much Michael's life changed. His new family hired him a tutor, worked hard to develop his interest in football, and gave him all the love, care, and support he never had before. As the story closes, Michael has made it all the way to college and then to professional football, playing for the Baltimore Ravens.

When people hear a story of a life changed, they are drawn to it, perhaps desperate to be a part of something like that. I believe this is something we *all* desire. We deeply want to make a difference in someone's life. We want to leave our mark and know that our life has counted for something. We want to do something bigger than ourselves.

We want to change the world.

At the movies we hear the story, feel good about it, maybe have a little cry, and then leave the theater and return to our normal lives—often lives that leave little room for making a difference in anything important at all. The problem is, we don't see the connection to what really has to happen to make a difference in someone's life. I am not sure if we really are *willing*, when push comes to shove, to do what is needed to change the world.

In *The Blind Side*, Michael's life did not magically change. He did not simply end up in the Tuohys' home or appear on that football field. He didn't just turn up at college one day. In order for Michael's life to truly change, someone had to take action, to step beyond a comfort zone and into another world. Someone had to take a risk. And someone had to have compassion.

To change a life, paths must cross and worlds must collide.

It was Christmas 1988. As my family sat in our living room, the phone rang. On the other end was our friend Donna, who lived in Brazil, working with orphaned and disadvantaged children. She was with us the day we found Nildo. Donna told us that someone special wanted to say hello.

A few moments later, Nildo wished us a merry Christmas and a happy new year. That was all his broken English allowed, so he quickly got off the phone and Donna got back on. She explained how she was visiting Rio de Janeiro for Christmas and visited one of our church partners there. When the pastor saw Donna, he asked her to come and greet the congregation.

After Donna walked onstage, she heard some commotion coming from the balcony. She looked up just in time to see a boy jump from the balcony to the main stage and charge toward her. It was Nildo.

When she reached down to give him a hug, she noticed that in one hand he had our family photo, and in the other hand he had the Bible we had all signed.

She paused, then told us, "He didn't know I was going to be there that day. He must carry those with him everywhere he goes!"

Nildo's story continues, and we share it often. As an adult, he lives in Brazil and works to help orphaned and abandoned children—children just like him. He is a living reminder of the words that well-meaning Brazilian pastor spoke so many years ago. I now know that I can't save them all . . . but *I can make a difference for one.*

Mother Teresa once said, "If I look at the mass I will never act. If I look at the one, I will."[9]

Nildo is a now a grown man, but when I look at his face today, I still see the face of that little five-year-old boy. I can't help but wonder what his life would have been like if we had not met that day.

What I think about even more is how different *my* life would have been if we had not met that day. Maybe I am the lucky one.

2

Comfortably Numb

You can't comfort the afflicted without afflicting the comfortable.

Princess Diana[1]

I sway back and forth. It is a beautiful summer day with a nice breeze. I look out over the water as I lie in a hammock a few feet away and rock back and forth . . . back and forth.

My eyes slowly close and my surroundings and thoughts start to fade as I watch boats cut through the water. The repetitive sound of the wake hitting the shore helps me slowly drift away as I continue to sway back and forth . . . back and forth.

I am lulled into a deep, peaceful sleep, and it feels wonderful.

For a few moments, I forget and escape everything—my problems, my anxiety, and all of my fears. I dream about only good things and forget the bad.

I become numb . . . comfortably numb.

Margarita and her mother stood in front of me with desperation in their eyes. Her mother held a plastic bag filled with some kind of paperwork.

I took years of Spanish in high school, but on that day I wish I had paid more attention and taken it more seriously, because I couldn't understand a word they said.

Cheryl, the wife of our partner in Guatemala, was with us, and I called her over to help me. She listened intently to the mother, and as she did, I saw the expression on her face drop. After years of living in Guatemala, Cheryl had seen more than her fair share of needs, but when I saw her tear up, I knew this was something more.

Cheryl explained that little Margarita had been raped. My heart sank. It's not that I don't know that things like this happen, but when the child is standing right in front of you, it takes on a whole new meaning. She was so little, so fragile, so innocent, and so pure. And she was only nine years old!

I was outraged. But there was more to the story.

Cheryl explained that the rape severely injured Margarita. She suffered major intestinal damage and had already undergone two surgeries to try to repair the injuries. My eyes began to well up with tears.

Margarita's mother gently pulled down her daughter's skirt, just enough for us to see the bandages on her stomach and the attached drainage bag. Her mother showed us the paperwork and medical records in the plastic bag she carried. She wanted us to know that she had done everything she could for her daughter. She wanted us to think she was a good mother. But she was out of money and resources, and she begged us for help.

Some might say this woman saw an opportunity. She knew Americans were coming to her village that day, and she took advantage of the situation. I say she did what any mother would do—what I would do—in that situation. She did everything in her power to make sure her little girl got the help she needed.

Think about the lengths you would go to get your child desperately needed help. I know that I wouldn't stop until I found help.

As I looked at the bandages on Margarita, I glanced around at the dirty, dusty village where she lived. She really didn't have a home at all. There were no walls for protection—only a tarp held up by a few sticks. Her village lacked access to running water or clean water of any kind. I wondered, "How does she keep her wounds clean? How does she avoid infection? How in the world has she survived—first the trauma of the rape and then two surgeries?"

Unfortunately, Margarita's story is not unique. It is retold around the world in vast numbers. The suffering is an epidemic.

It is a story I have heard many times.

"There are three [children] in all," the woman said. "They are all infected. The mother is infected. These kids are suffering. There's nothing at all. They've got no clothing. They've got no food. There's no income at home, because the mother is sick. No one is helping them." As I listened, I almost felt guilty for my life, my own health, and my family's health.

Because the traumatized little girl didn't talk much, the kind lady who found Jamira told me her story. The little girl walked up shyly and never looked me in the eyes. A quiet ten-year-old, Jamira was one of hundreds of children we met in a rural village of South Africa. All of the women and children who crowded in and around the small, dust-filled, concrete compound were affected by AIDS. All were extremely poor, and most had been abandoned.

As we talked with Jamira and the others, I thought about how foreign it all seemed to me. These children knew nothing but extreme poverty. Every meal was a struggle. Attending school was a privilege, not an assumption. Suffering was a daily part of life. Many of them had never lived a day without the effects of AIDS.

I soon discovered the reason for Jamira's withdrawn disposition—this little girl had been raped by her mother's boyfriend. The monster had infected her with HIV!

Jamira's spirit was crushed.

When I heard about the torture this child endured in her own home, I wanted to put my arms around her to protect her. I knew this child's pain ran deeper than the disease that invaded her little body, and I wanted to take that all away.

Brokenhearted, I could only imagine how Jamira must live in fear and shame. How was she supposed to trust anyone? Her violation was not by a stranger but by someone her own mother had allowed into her life.

I fought back the tears, then hugged Jamira. How I wished I could take her pain away. I knew I would never forget her.

Jamira and her family are among millions who live with the pain and impact of AIDS and its daily, never-ending toll.

I remember when AIDS first moved into the global spotlight. I wrote a speech on AIDS for a competition in high school. It was the new, hot topic, and we knew so little about it. I researched and wrote down words that I would say, but they were just words. I never realized that years later I would come face-to-face with AIDS.

No one could have imagined what a short time it would take for AIDS to have a devastating impact on people across the globe. The most obvious impact of this plague is the death count. Now as AIDS hits thirty years, an estimated 30 million people worldwide have already died.[2] Unbelievable! I can hardly fathom that staggering number. Deaths in sub-Saharan Africa alone are expected to reach 55 million by 2020.[3]

Those of us who are fortunate to live in a nation that is not completely engulfed by AIDS sometimes have a hard time relating to those who live in such a desperate state. After meeting child after child like Jamira, I began to think, "What a different world from mine." But then something happened that changed my mind and heart.

A railroad track ran near the building where we met in South Africa. Right in the middle of our visit, we heard the deep rumble and piercing horn of an approaching train. Boys from across the compound ran to the chain-link fence, lined up with excitement, and hooked their fingers into the fence as they watched the mighty train rush past. They laughed and gestured with glee as it roared by. Their excitement made me smile, because I remembered the same reaction to trains from my own children. Boys will be boys no matter whether they are born in Virginia or South Africa. Boys just like trains.

> "I would rather feel compassion than know the meaning of it."
>
> Thomas Aquinas[4]

As I watched, I saw those children for who they were—children just like my own, boys and girls like those we love. They feel, they love, they hurt, just like you and me. The only difference is that their families and communities live with a plague that devours all they hold dear.

Coming home from Africa, I sat on the plane pondering all I had seen. I wondered how I could ever explain the sights, smells, and stories. It was all too much. While in Africa doing research for a book on children affected by AIDS, I spent every day interviewing women and children whose lives had been torn apart, but I had no idea how I could really explain what I had seen. A book would be difficult enough to write, but in that moment, I wondered how I could explain it even to my friends and family. It is not the kind of topic one brings up at lunch with girlfriends.

Over the years, when I have tried to talk to people about the incredible needs around the world, too often I've seen their eyes glaze over. They can't take it all in, so it's easier to ignore. Sometimes I feel like Charlie Brown's teacher. I feel like all they hear me saying is "Wa-wa, wa-wa, wa-wa."

Unfortunately, many times this causes me to say nothing at all. There's so much to say, but I can't speak. My heart is heavy; the situations are just too hard to explain.

People talk about culture shock. I have never experienced that when going on such trips, but I always experience it coming home. It is called "reentry." "Over there" things are simple and clear. The needs are great and at times overwhelming, but the big, hard questions become easy to answer. What is crucial in life—what matters and what doesn't—becomes clear when you deal with life and death issues.

But in America, things are less than clear, at best. CNN news anchor Anderson Cooper said it this way:

> Coming home meant coming down. It was easier to stay up. I'd return home to piles of bills and an empty refrigerator. Buying groceries, I'd get lost—too many aisles, too many choices; cool mist blowing over fresh fruit; paper or plastic; cash back in return? I wanted emotion but couldn't find it here. . . . I'd come back and couldn't speak the language. Out there the pain is palpable; you breathed it in the air. Back here, no one talked about life and death. No one seemed to understand.[5]

The day I returned from that trip to Africa, I went to a baseball game with my family. I know part of my emotions was jet lag, but I remember sitting there thinking about all I had just seen in Africa, everything I experienced. I looked around and wondered, "Why doesn't anyone feel like I feel?"

The beer and peanuts flowed that day at America's favorite pastime. People yelled and screamed at the players and umpire. The mascot danced on top of the dugout, people fought over foul balls, and the crowd sang "Take Me Out to the Ball Game."

It was a normal day at the park, but that day, it just hit me.

Do these people not know that 42 million people are suffering with AIDS and that 70 percent of them are in Africa?[6] Do they not know that 16.6 million children have been orphaned by AIDS?[7] Do they not know that an entire continent is wasting away while we are playing baseball?

Don't they know? Don't they care? Have we become comfortably numb?

Please don't misunderstand me here. There is nothing wrong with baseball; my boys would strongly object to me saying otherwise. I have nine- and thirteen-year-old sons, so baseball is a big part of my life right now, and I would have it no other way.

Baseball is not my point. The point is, our lives are filled with so many distractions—some good and some bad, but distractions just the same. If we choose, we can live our whole life so filled with these distractions that we never have to face—or be confronted with—real, desperate needs.

Maybe the question is, can we even comprehend issues like AIDS and poverty? Do we fully grasp that more than one billion people in the world don't live like we do? Is our Starbucks, iPhone, Twitter, Facebook, flat-screen TV, and all-you-can-eat buffet lifestyle just too far removed from the lives of the poor?

Can we even begin to understand what it would be like to helplessly watch a child die? To watch your own child die because you don't have any food or you can't afford to visit the doctor or there is no doctor? Do we really get that?

The pain, poverty, sickness, and hunger that I have witnessed around the world is almost too much to bear. I have talked to women abandoned by husbands who left them infected with HIV. I have hugged children who lost both parents and are now all alone. I have cried with young girls who were raped, their innocence lost. Extreme hunger, poverty, and disease—it is devastating.

Sometimes I can't wait to get home, back to my life, family, and world—the real world.

But the world we live in is not the real world. We live in a bubble, a world more like Disneyland. The rest of the world is reality.

It's said that the first step toward battling addiction is admitting you have a problem. In the same way, I say the first step toward changing the world is admitting there is a problem. We may do that briefly, but we are quickly convinced we can't do anything about it.

We have been lulled into a deep sleep, and we need to wake up.

Bill Hybels writes in his book *Holy Discontent* that we need to figure out what we can't stand. Most people try to avoid this process, but the truth is, there is something in the world that bothers you. There's something you can't stand. Is it the issue of poverty, injustice, prejudice, the homeless, or abandoned children?

> "The poor do not need our sympathy and our pity, the poor need our love and compassion."
>
> Mother Teresa[8]

Once you find what you can't stand—what disturbs you—you have to feed it. In other words, increase your exposure to it. If you are not careful, you will fill your life with other things so that you don't have to pay attention to what wrecks you. You will medicate your discontent.[9]

Most likely, you will be perfectly content to stay numb. Our society as a whole is numb, and we are pathetically comfortable. John Stott puts it this way:

> The horror of the situation is that our affluent culture has drugged us; we no longer feel the pain of other people's deprivations. Yet the first step toward the recovery of our Christian integrity is to be aware that our culture blinds, deafens and dopes us. Then we shall begin to cry to God to open our eyes, unstop our ears and stab our dull consciences awake, until we see, hear and feel what through his Word he has been saying to us all the time. Then we shall take action.[10]

Margarita is now thriving. My family helped provide the last surgery she needed. It was extensive. The doctors said they had to completely reconstruct her internally. That is hard for me to even comprehend, but I am so grateful she now has a chance to lead a normal life.

Through the help of some others who met her on that same trip, she now has a new home to live in with her family. A home to feel safe and protected in.

One life . . . completely changed. One life . . . saved.

I know what wrecks me, and I can't be numb to it anymore. It is just too hard. I want to see the needs. I want to feel the needs. I want to touch them.

3

Eyes Glued Shut

I saw what I saw and I can't forget it
I heard what I heard and I can't go back
I know what I know and I can't deny it
Something on the road cut me to the soul
I say what I say with no hesitation
I have what I have and I'm giving it up
I do what I do with deep conviction
Something on the road changed my world

Sara Groves[1]

had just fallen asleep when I was suddenly awakened by my husband. I instantly knew something was terribly wrong. I asked him what happened and he could barely tell me. I really think he didn't want to tell me, but he had no choice.

He had been up late and randomly decided to try to glue back together some sunglasses that he had broken. He got out some superglue to solve the problem. He was having some trouble getting the glue out of the tube, so he squeezed harder . . . and harder . . . and harder . . . well, I think you get the picture. The tube exploded and superglue went flying straight into his eyes. Before he knew it, his eyes were quickly sticking together and closing shut.

I grabbed the kids and rushed him to the emergency room in the middle of the night. I sat in the car waiting, not knowing whether to laugh or cry. He ended up being fine—just a little embarrassed. At the time, it was very scary, but right now as I am writing about it, I am having a hard time not laughing. We left the hospital that night feeling thankful, and with the most expensive pair of sunglasses anyone has ever owned.

I use this story to say this: we would never intentionally glue our eyes shut. But we seem to do it every day.

Just like watching a horror film, too often we cover our eyes. We choose and control how much we see and peek out from behind the pillow only if and when we want to.

We live with our heads in the sand.

We turn the channel, look the other way, and fill our lives with so many distractions that we never really have to face reality. But that does not make the evil go away. Albert Einstein once said, "The world is a dangerous place, not because of those who do evil, but because of those who look on and do nothing."[2]

Our eyes see so much junk that we almost close them shut until we can no longer see the harsh truth. We need to flush them out so that we can once again see clearly.

In the blockbuster film *Avatar*, the Na'vi greet each other with the words "I see you." But this simple and obvious statement is meant to communicate much more. Blogger Vijayendra Mohanty wrote, "What this acknowledgement means is simply empathy. It means that you acknowledge the other as one like yourself. It means that the 'I' and the 'You' are the same—parts of a bigger whole. . . . What this awareness does is that it makes the individual recognise his place in the world. It makes him humble . . . and it makes him care for the world around him."[3] And as another columnist explained, this phrase means, "I see myself, in your eyes."[4]

Now, I am not buying into the religion of *Avatar*, just using it to make this point: We see people—but how often do we *really* see them? Do we see ourselves in their eyes? Do we see ourselves in their pain?

We see their stories on television; we read about them in magazines and in the paper. But do we really "see them"? I believe if we did, we would be outraged. We would not be able to go back to life as usual. We would accept why we were created and what our purpose is—our greater purpose. And we would act on those feelings.

Black hair . . . all I could see was black hair. Rows and rows of children filed in for the assembly, and sitting high on the stage overlooking the crowd, I saw something I had never seen before. Hundreds of students had gathered together at the same time, and all with the same color hair!

I was only eleven years old, and I was on my first trip overseas. I went all by myself—well, almost. My dad was there too, but that really didn't count. He pretty much let me do what I wanted and gave me lots of freedom. What my mom didn't know wouldn't hurt her!

My best friend and I were so excited to be on our first "mission trip" to Korea and the Philippines. We were the youngest ones on the trip. The rest of the group was made up of college students, our dads, and a few other adult staff. We enjoyed acting older than we really were and hanging out with the college kids.

On this particular day we were holding an assembly at a large South Korean school. Looking out onto that crowd, I began to realize what a big world we live in—and how small I really am.

We left the school and visited the DMZ (Korean Demilitarized Zone). This 156-mile-long strip of land serves as a buffer between North and South Korea. The DMZ is two and a half miles wide and is heavily guarded and lined with barbed wire and land mines.[5] I walked in a building where if you stand on one side of the room you are in South Korea, and on the other side of the room you are in North Korea. But my most vivid memory of this visit is the propaganda. Standing in South Korea, looking over into North Korea, you could not escape the sound coming from the loudspeakers blaring propaganda messages. Promises of prosperity were made to anyone who would come to North Korea. It was eerie. The North Koreans had even gone to the trouble of creating a facade of a town that you could see from the South Korean side. They made it appear very nice and luxurious, but telescopes revealed only empty shells of buildings. It was not a real town at all. Any hope of prosperity in North Korea was a lie then and is a lie even today.

The 2011 World Watch List of countries where Christians are most likely to be persecuted for their faith is topped once again by North Korea, for the ninth year in a row![6] North Korea is home to thousands of Christians who are brutally attacked, forced out of jobs, removed from their homes, imprisoned, tortured, or even killed, just because of their faith. It's difficult to imagine a place filled with such desperation, fear, cruelty, domination, and lack of basic human rights. But without question, North Korea, a communist nation of 20 million, is one of the most hostile places on earth.

On that day years ago, I was able to clearly see the line between freedom and communism, between hope and despair, between light and darkness . . . between good and evil.

At the age of thirteen, Evah had already lived through more pain and terror than many of us endure in our entire lives. Born in a remote village in Uganda, Evah lived in a small hut with her family and grew up like most of the children in the area. She loved her mother and father very much. They were all very happy, until a dark night that would change her life forever.

One moment Evah, who was eleven years old at the time, lay snug in her bed with the rhythmic noises of the village at night lulling her to sleep. In the next instant, the crack of gunfire mixed with yelling and screaming jolted her awake into a living nightmare. Scary, shadowy figures violently stormed into her family's hut.

They were members of the dreaded Lord's Resistance Army (LRA), hordes of cold-blooded murderers. The rebel LRA soldiers murdered Evah's father and severely beat her mother. Then they turned their fury onto the child. They dragged the frightened girl out of the hut and hit her over and over again, telling her they would kill her if she did not do as she was told.

The rebels forced her to carry a weapon and ammunition for their army. She was raped and soon became pregnant by one of the soldiers. Evah had a baby when she was only twelve years old—just a child herself! But then the absolutely unthinkable happened: Evah was forced to watch as the soldiers shot and killed her baby.

"You, LORD, hear the desire of the afflicted;
   you encourage them, and you listen to their cry, defending the fatherless and the oppressed,
   so that mere earthly mortals will never again strike terror.

Ps. 10:17–18

After they killed her baby, Evah tried to escape. She was captured and once again severely beaten—she suffered more than a hundred lashes. Despite the dangerous consequences, Evah fled again and finally got away. When she returned home, she found her mother had been stabbed by the rebels and had gone insane. Evah was left with no one to care for her and no one to comfort her as she struggled with nightmares and memories.

Evah is just one of the thousands of children abducted by Joseph Kony and his LRA. Since 1986, more than 40,000 children ages seven to seventeen have been abducted to be used as child soldiers and slaves.[7] At the height of the rebel attacks, over 40,000 children, some as young as five years old, left their villages to take refuge in towns for the night and make the trek back home the next morning.[8] Many walked as far as eight miles each way on their dangerous commute. They had no choice but to flee. These boys and girls were not safe in their own beds.

The danger of these attacks displaced 1.8 million people, and many of them ended up in Internally Displaced Persons (IDP) camps.[9] I visited one of these camps in northern Uganda and witnessed the horrible conditions. Hundreds of children roamed the dirty spaces between huts. Some were clothed in rags; others had no clothes at all. Many of them were starving. Others were dying from AIDS and other painful diseases.

I met the director of the Palenga IDP Camp in Gulu. At the time he told me that this camp housed 17,000 of these displaced people, and of those, an estimated 40 percent were HIV positive, though most didn't even know it. As I walked through the camp with the director, the sights and smells were unbearable. The huts were so close together that we literally had to turn our bodies sideways to get through. He led us to the highest point of the camp, and from there the sight was unbelievable: thatched-roof huts as far as you could see in every direction.

Walking back, I began asking the director some basic questions: What is your name? Are you married? Do you have any children? I wish I had not asked that last question. If I could have taken it back, I would have. But it was too late, and his answer still haunts me today.

He explained that four years prior, his son and daughter were abducted by the LRA. His son was only eleven at the time. His daughter was thirteen. They were taken in the middle of the night at gunpoint. Two months later they found his son, who had managed to escape after weeks of torture.

He told me, "They have not found my daughter yet." That last word *yet* is important because that is how he answered the question—with hope, even after four years. I can't even begin to imagine his anguish.

Evil creates great fear and sorrow, but those who endure can also inspire incredible hope. I can't help but remember the voices of children from a church and children's center that we supported in this same area of Gulu, Uganda. As we arrived, these children whose families have been torn apart by poverty, HIV/AIDS, and a twenty-year civil war ran to greet us—smiling, laughing, and offering handshakes and hugs. Each boy and girl is special and unique. They are children who without our support would not have the opportunity to attend school, a place where they also receive at least one nutritious meal a day. This is a privilege for them and not something they take for granted.

I watched them in their red-and-green school uniforms play a game that looked somewhat familiar, like "Duck, Duck, Goose" with an African twist. Then the children formed a large circle and began to chant a poem together. I had to listen carefully to understand what they were saying, but once I did, my heart stopped. This is what they called out over and over again:

> Who is a child?
> A child is a person below eighteen.
> What do they need?
> Love, care, comfort.
> They are young and innocent.
> Give them protection.
> They need protection.

How can we turn a deaf ear to such a cry for help? If I listen, I can hear them still:

> What do they need?
> Love, care, comfort.

Rani was only seven years old when her life changed forever. As a poor family in India, Rani's parents struggled to give their daughter the kinds of opportunities they wanted her to have. When a relative offered to take Rani in and give her an education, her parents reluctantly agreed. They were promised they could visit whenever they wanted. But the day Rani left her home was one of the last days her parents ever saw her.

Rani was caught in a trap that captures millions of young women and children around the world every day. She was sold into slavery and abused and mistreated until she was once again sold. But this time she was sold into adoption. An unsuspecting, kind woman brought Rani into her loving home in America.

It was years later before Rani could remember everything that had happened to her in India. Once she remembered, she traveled back to find her birth mother, and amazingly, she found her.

I met Rani last year and heard her tell her inspiring story firsthand. Even at just five-foot-seven, I towered over Rani. But don't let her short stature fool you. She is one powerful and passionate woman. Through her Tronie Foundation, she is determined to save other children from the life she was forced to endure. The foundation focuses on promoting anti-trafficking education, policy change, and restoration for trafficking survivors. Rani networks with stars and celebrities like Demi Moore and Mira Sorvino. She was the recipient of the 2008 UN Human Rights Award, and the United Nations asked her to travel the world representing the cause of ending human trafficking. Her story was even featured on *Oprah*.[10]

But this passionate woman has a daunting task ahead of her. It is reported that human trafficking is the fastest growing means by which people are enslaved, the fastest growing international crime, and one of the largest sources of income for organized crime.[11] Every year, 1.2 million children are trafficked, and human trafficking has become the second largest source of illegal income worldwide, exceeded only by drug trafficking.[12] In fact, it is suspected to be a 32-billion-dollar-a-year industry.[13]

The reality is that many of these numbers are low. The perpetrators of these crimes are not exactly handing in reports. Regardless, more people are enslaved today than were during the whole of the trans-Atlantic African slave trade.[14]

I knew about slavery and trafficking before I met Rani. But after I met her, it became real, and it became personal. I "saw" her and I "saw" the need. And I love her spirit. In a briefing to the UN, she quoted these words from Ghandi: "When I despair, I remember that all through history the ways of truth and love have always won. There have been tyrants, and murderers, and for a time they can seem invincible, but in the end they always fall. Think of it—always."[15]

Doing what I do means that I hear incredible stories and see incredible needs every day. It can be overwhelming at times—sometimes I just want to turn it off. I laugh because quite often I feel like "Debbie Downer" from *Saturday Night Live*. They open this sketch with a funny song about "Debbie Downer," saying she is "always here to tell you about a new disease, a car accident, or killer bees."

No matter what fun and happy topic people are discussing in these sketches, Debbie Downer always interjects the most depressing comments. If they are talking about birthday wishes, she says something like, "If I had a wish, I wish that they would release that poor hostage in Iraq." If they are talking about going fishing, she says something like, "Oh, count me out. My doctor says if I don't cut down on fish, my mercury levels may reach a toxic level." And no matter what the topic, she will add this: "Did you know that feline AIDS is the number one killer of domestic animals?" Every time she adds one of these conversation killers, the music in the background sounds like *"wah-wah."*[16]

As funny as I think this sketch is on *SNL*, it kind of reminds me of my own life. Too often I have shied away from sharing stories with friends and family because they do seem like those "Debbie Downer" conversation killers. I remember coming home from Africa with my heart so full of what I had seen. I could speak to a group of people about it, but one-on-one with friends or a group of women didn't work so well. It is much easier to block out the evil in our world, and no one wants to be a "Debbie Downer."

We don't deal with life and death on a daily basis here, and talking about it makes us extremely uncomfortable. But maybe in order to truly live, we have to truly face the evil.

> "If you don't like the way the world is, you change it. You have an obligation to change it. You just do it one step at a time."
>
> Marian Wright Edelman[17]

You know that sick feeling you get when you see a photo of yourself and in one moment, your image is shattered? Before you saw the photo, you didn't know you looked like that. You had an idea in your mind of what you looked like—an idea that you were happy with. But after you see the photo, you are forced to look at yourself differently and deal with the consequences. So it is with evil. Once you have seen it, you have to deal with the consequences.

You don't have to look far to find examples of evil—it's all around us. It is in our own country and in our own neighborhoods. Remember Jaycee Dugard? She was only eleven when she was kidnapped while waiting for her school bus. She spent the next eighteen years in the backyard of a known, violent sex offender who repeatedly abused and raped her. These attacks produced two daughters who played in the yard for anyone to see. Even though police checked the house as part of the man's parole, and even though they were called to the house on a report that he had children living with him, they never checked the backyard. Neighbors suspected something was not quite right but hesitated to get involved. In this case, evil lived right under our noses—or right in our backyard.

I once saw a story on *Oprah* that literally made me nauseated. I could barely take it. It was about a beautiful six-year-old boy named Clayton. His parents would lock him up in a small closet, wrap a wire fence around him, and chain him to it. They would leave him there for hours and even days. I listened to tapes of the boy telling the police what it was like when he was locked up and how he could not sit down or lie down to rest or go to sleep. He was thirsty, hungry, and terrified.

Let's face it: there is evil all around us. But somehow we have also found some easy ways to escape it. We can change the channel, drive to the other side of town, go shopping, leave for vacation—all to escape. Maybe there is evil right under our noses and we are just too busy to see it. Or maybe there is evil half a world away, and we just choose not to see it.

As Ravi Zacharias said, "Evil is not just where blood has been spilled. Evil is in the self-absorbed human heart."[18]

After coming home from Africa, Jim Palmer said it this way in his book *Divine Nobodies*:

> Somewhere over the Atlantic, forty thousand feet above the earth, these nice thoughts about God gave way to disturbing images I wish I could forget from my trip. Now the question, "Where was God today?" tortured me. Today, a ten-year-old girl is being strapped down tight to a bed and brutally and repeatedly raped. God is present. Today an eight-year-old emaciated boy is covered with a cardboard box and left to die. Slowly he slips into unconsciousness. God is present. Today a young mom of three wails in bed as her skeletal body writhes with the unrelenting agony of AIDS. God is present. Still I grew angry. Why was God pushing all these horrors in my face? I was emotionally spent and wanted to go home to my world. God could have that world; that was his deal, he's God; I didn't live in that world. Or did I? Sitting in 13D, I uncovered something unsettling about myself. I don't really

41

want a "relationship" with God. Here's what I want. I want to share with God all I feel, all I need, all that grieves me, all that makes me happy, the puzzling things, the hard things, but I would prefer that God keeps his stuff to himself. I don't want to hear about his pain and grief.[19]

I have often said that if we really want to know God, we have to be willing to know everything about him. Not just the pretty stuff. Not just the stuff that is easy. Not just the stuff that makes us feel good. We have to be willing to embrace all that God is about, all that he loves, and all that breaks his heart.

Too often we want to settle for a God who knows and loves everything about us. A God who takes care of us, who makes all our dreams come true, and who keeps us safe. And we are comfortable letting God keep the hurt and pain in the far corners of the world all to himself. He can keep all of that; just let us keep living in our world—our cool, clean, comfortable world.

We usually think of evil as something morally bad or wrong and coming from an evil tyrant. But it can also refer to the social evils of poverty and injustice. Evil can simply be defined as the opposite of good.

I was reminded of the social evils of poverty and injustice by my friend Brittany Hilker. She has worked for the past few years with Danita's Children, an organization helping thousands of orphaned children and families in Northern Haiti. In the days following the 2010 earthquake, she was on the front lines rescuing children from the rubble in Port-au-Prince. She has seen the worst pain and suffering imaginable and has responded with great compassion.

Because of my work with cause*life* (a movement of people dedicated to provide the most essential need to human life—water), I am very much aware of the need for clean water around the world and the effect dirty water has, especially on children.

But Brittany's story reminded me of the true life-and-death nature of this global problem. She shared about a little baby boy named Wesnerson who recently died from the effects of dirty water—an unnecessary death. Here is an excerpt of his story:

Life is different here. Death is different. It's everywhere, it's unnecessary, and the worst part is that it's almost always preventable. I woke up early yesterday morning to set aside more time to pray and be with the Lord. I knew He was going to teach me something that day. I asked Him to show me His heart . . . and He showed me His hurt.

Yesterday Karris called me. She said our friend's baby was on the property and was really, really sick. I had seen him last week, I knew he was sick, but she put the phone up to his mouth so I could hear his labored breathing; he had never been that sick before. She said it was serious. Mya was taking care of him as I got there. She was praying over him as he lay lifeless a few steps away from the construction of our clinic. "I think this baby just died," she said. We decided to rush him to the hospital to see if he could be saved. I took the baby in my arms and got on the back of a motorcycle taxi. He was lifeless, but his eyes were partly open. I hoped that meant he was still hanging on. As the taxi driver raced down the road, I prayed and screamed for life to come back into this sweet little baby. His head still hung heavy in my arms as I ran through the clinic, kicking in the doors of the doctor's offices, yelling for someone to help. There were no doctors. I ran to the nurses' office, yelled for help, and said that I didn't know if the baby was dead or alive. A lady slowly looked up at me, said to wait in the next room over. She listened for a heartbeat and felt the boy's limp body. "He's already cold," she said. "He's dead."

I asked for a sheet. They left me alone with the baby for a while, came back a few minutes later to wrap him up, put two

> "If you think you're too small to make a difference, you haven't been in bed with a mosquito."
>
> Anita Roddick[20]

pieces of tape around him, and then left. What do you do with a dead baby? There's no hospital morgue, no ambulance, no parents; just me and a room full of curious people who I'm sure have seen this same scene way too many times before. I took the dead baby in my arms, still as careful with his body as I would be if he was alive. I couldn't even remember his name. Shame on me; I'd been helping this family for months. They came every 15 days to get money and food. Louis, the father, lost his wife in the earthquake and was taking care of his two children on his own. He lost everything in the earthquake, got on a bus not knowing where it was going, and got off at the last stop, which was our town. He wandered the streets until a loving Haitian woman took him and his children in.

I'll never get used to seeing grown men collapse to the ground as they find out their child has died. And I will never get used to babies dying from something as curable as diarrhea. His name was Wesnerson, although his family called him Kevens—it's a name his older brother gave him. Another face the world will never know. As he was dead in my arms, I believe he was alive in our Savior's.

I ask God every day to show me who He is. It's a dangerous request if you aren't ready for it. Because God is joy and love and all those good things, but to really know God is to know Him in His pain too. God loses a child every day. He sees things we don't see. You can change the channel when you see a starving child commercial, and I can pass by their house every day, but God knows that child intimately . . . they are His. A father who, every day, has to watch his children die all alone, in a little mud hut with no one to even cry over them. My friend Karris has been here eight years and she always gives a better perspective on the suffering we see here. She reminded me that God didn't let this baby die alone. He died with all of us fighting for him. He died . . . right in front of the clinic (we) are building for this very reason . . . so we can stop having to say, "I'm sorry" to 15-pound corpses. Yesterday I got a small glimpse of His hurt. We don't usually think of God as having feelings or pain, but I believe His heart breaks far more easily than ours does. My prayer is to know God's heart; both in His joy and in His pain.[21]

We couldn't save Wesnerson in time, but we can change the future. As I write this, a complete water system is being built in Ouanaminthe, Haiti. This will be one of the only clean water sources in a community of over 110,000 people. Children's lives will literally be saved every day with this fresh, clean water.

A few years back, I had some photos on the wall of my office. They were of two boys who had been part of our child sponsorship program. Although the young boys did not know each other, they shared something horrible in common. During the same time period, they both committed suicide. Our help had come too late, and their traumatic childhoods proved too much to bear.

I kept their photos on my wall for some time to serve as a reminder. I wanted to "see"—I wanted to remember. If we truly see, then we really can help. We are not going to win every single battle, but sometimes the ones we lose inspire us the most.

I have seen the evil in the world, and if you are honest, so have you. But it is true that "The greatest and most shameful regrets of history are always about the truth we failed to tell."[22]

When we stand before God one day, will we really say that we didn't know? Will we really say that we didn't see the needs of our world—that we chose to look away? What will our excuse be for not getting involved?

4

The Meaning of Enough

In my own little world it hardly ever rains
I've never gone hungry and always felt safe
I got some money in my pocket, shoes on
*   my feet*
In my own little world
Population me

Matthew West[1]

Pineapple is my favorite fruit, and I suppose it is my favorite story too. Let me explain: as a child, I loved a book called *The Pineapple Story*. Never heard of it? I am not surprised. This was a short book, just a little over thirty pages long. It was a missionary classic published in 1978, and it was "old school" in every sense of the phrase. But for some reason this book, with its primitive one-color drawings, fascinated me. I am not sure how many times my parents read it to me and how many times I read it to myself, but it never got old.

It was a true story about a missionary who lived in the bush of what was then called Dutch New Guinea. In the jungle where he lived, he longed for fresh fruit, so he decided to plant pineapples. However, this was no quick fix. It would take three years for the plants to yield any fruit.

He hired one of the local men to plant the pineapples for him and paid him for the days he worked. After three years, the pineapples were beginning to ripen, but before the missionary and his family could eat any of them, the locals would steal them. Just as each one became ripe, it would be quickly stolen.

He and his wife were shocked. Here they were, missionaries, trying to help these people. They had a clinic to take care of their sick and give them medicine, and they had a store to help supply their basic needs like salt, matches, and fish hooks. But it did not matter. They still stole all the pineapples.

He finally found out that the person responsible for stealing the pineapples was the very man who had helped plant them. He confronted the man about this, but his response was, "My hands plant them. My mouth eats them." This was the rule of the jungle, and they did not understand any other rule. The missionary tried to negotiate by offering him half of the pineapple plants—but the pineapples were still stolen. He then offered them the whole garden. He said he would plant a new one and they both could have their own pineapples. But it was all to no avail. In frustration, he decided to pay someone to root up all the plants, throw them out, and start all over again. That way the locals would have no right to the new plants.

This time he negotiated from the very beginning, explaining that the locals would be planting the pineapples and that he would pay them for their work. But when the pineapples were ripe, he and his family would eat them. Everything was clear, or so he thought.

Three long years passed again, and the pineapples began to ripen. But the negotiation had not worked after all, and every night more and more pineapples were stolen. To retaliate, he decided to close the store where everyone got their supplies. This worked, but only because all the people left the village. They had no reason to live there without the supplies. So now this missionary was all alone with no one to serve.

He reopened the store, and the people returned. But then he got a big dog to protect the pineapples. This worked as well, but the people were scared of the dog, so they quit coming around. And once again, he had no one to serve and no one to help him learn the language.

I guess you could say that this was where the missionary hit rock bottom. And that was when he changed his plan. He stood out in the garden one night praying and said this: "Lord, see these pineapple bushes? I have fought to have fruit from them. I have claimed them. I have stood up for my rights. It is all wrong and I realize it now. I have seen that it is wrong and I give them to you. From now on, if you want me to eat any of your pineapples, fine. You just go right ahead and give them to us. If not, fine. It doesn't really matter."[3]

> "It is poverty to decide that a child must die so that you may live as you wish."
> Mother Teresa[2]

Well, even after this heartfelt prayer, the pineapples continued to be stolen. But this time his response was different. The locals came to him and asked if he had become a Christian. He couldn't believe what he was hearing. He had been a Christian for twenty years—he was a missionary! But it was hard to argue with them when they told him that the reason they thought he had become a Christian was because he did not get angry anymore when they stole his pineapples. Wow, that had to hurt.

When he explained that the reason he did not get angry anymore was because they were not his pineapples but God's, the people thought twice about stealing. Instead, when the pineapples became ripe, they came and told the missionary, and they all were able to eat them and share them together.

Finally the missionary had exactly what he had wanted all along—pineapples *and* people who were willing to hear about his faith. His faith was now authentic and something that they could believe in.[4]

This story from my childhood still has something to teach me today. I find it interesting that sometimes the very thing that we can use to make a difference in people's lives around the world is also the very thing we are not willing to give up. It is the thing that we hold on to so tightly but yet the thing that has the power to make a difference.

Money is the easy answer here, but too often money is really not the problem. More often fear, complacency, and culture are what hold us back.

A couple years ago on a flight headed to the West Coast, I sat next to a man who was very talkative. Now, you need to know that my preference while traveling is to sit back, relax, and hopefully fall asleep. I am most happy when I am next to an empty seat or someone like me who keeps to themselves and falls asleep shortly into the flight.

But on this particular flight, it was obvious that quickly falling asleep was not going to be an option. Paul was a nice businessman traveling home, and he was very interested in my work around the world. I have to admit, I enjoyed our conversation.

Paul told me about a man who had made a great impact on his life. Although he had passed away, it was obvious what he had meant to Paul and how much he had taught him. Paul shared with me a very simple yet poignant question that his mentor had asked him one day. He said, "What would be the reward for the person who knew the meaning of enough?"

I couldn't get this thought out of my head for the rest of the weekend—the meaning of enough. How do you put that into words?

I arrived in Dallas and joined our Children of the World International Children's Choir at a church where we were sharing the stage with Kay Warren. Kay is the wife of Rick

Warren, a megachurch pastor and author of the bestseller *The Purpose Driven Life*. That weekend Kay shared a powerful message of her struggle with cancer—a struggle that came at an unexpected time in her life. It was a time when she was doing so much for God and taking on the issue of AIDS in a very big way. Kay shared that "we can't control *how long* we live, but we can control *how* we live." So simple, so true, and yet so hard to live by each and every day.

I began to see how these two simple thoughts actually fit together. If we really understood the meaning of enough, we would choose to live very differently. We would use our resources to help more people instead of buying more things for ourselves. We would be satisfied with what we have instead of always wanting more. We would lead a very different life.

I heard a Spanish word recently that caught my attention: *dejar*. It means to let go, abandon, leave behind, or forget. If only we could let go of the things that inhibit us from being who we were meant to be. So many distractions keep us from being who we were meant to be and doing what we were meant to do.

In the months following the tragic earthquake in Haiti, I had many discussions with people about the needs affecting that country. Some recurring themes in these conversations were comments like, "Haiti was so poor even before the earthquake," "They had so many problems before the earthquake—big problems," and of course, "We have tried to help Haiti before. It never makes a difference."

There is some truth in each of these statements. The long-term issues of poverty are complex, and there are no simple answers. But the problem of a hungry and thirsty child is a simple one to solve and one that we can change.

Max Lucado says in his book *Outlive Your Life*, "He [Jesus] values a level playing field. In his society, the Have-a-Lots and the Have-a-Littles are never to be so far apart that they can't see each other." Then he goes on to say, "In the game of life, many of us who cross home plate do so because we were born on third base. Others aren't even on a team."[5]

Speaking from the world of the Have-a-Lots who cross home plate every day, I think we can agree that the distance between us and the Have-a-Littles in Haiti and around the world is vast . . . too vast. And it is within our power to make a difference.

The richest areas of the world are no surprise: Western Europe, North America, Australia, and Japan. And the poorest areas are where you would think as well: sub-Saharan Africa, India, and Southeast Asia.[6] According to the World Institute for Development Economics Research, "The wealth share estimates reveal that the richest 2 percent of adult individuals own more than half of all global wealth, with the richest 1 percent alone accounting for 40 per cent of global assets. . . . In contrast, the bottom half of wealth holders together hold barely 1 percent of global wealth." Here's the shocking part: you need only about $2,140 to your name (assets minus debts) to be counted among the wealthiest 50 percent of the world.[7]

Worldwide, 1 out of every 2 children lives in the most desperate poverty conditions.[8] Over 925 million people worldwide suffer from malnutrition.[9] Ninety-eight percent of those live in developing countries and 104 million are young children.[10]

The world's poorest 1.4 billion people live on less than $1.25 a day.[11]

I met a young man in South Africa named Thando. He was a child of poverty, but a child who had found his way to the other side. Growing up in the shacks of Cape Town was a harsh life that didn't cut him any breaks. Thando was an orphan who survived not only life alone in the slums but also a deadly fire that left scars on his face and hands that remain even today. I remember Thando poignantly sharing with me, "It's hard to hold on to your dreams when you don't have food to eat."

Most days I don't have to worry about having food to eat unless I have just neglected getting to the grocery store. In fact, most days I am trying to figure out how I can try to eat less. If food is keeping me from my dreams, it is only the dream of looking great in a swimsuit.

One day I visited a dump in Guatemala where desperate children and families come searching for food—anything they can find. When they can't find food, they look for broken pieces of glass. When they fill a bag full of glass, they can sell it for the equivalent of a quarter. It will take them nearly all day to fill a bag.

I simply cannot describe the smell in this place. It was 105 degrees on the day I was there, and the heat intensified the already horrible odors. It was a place you would never want to be at all, let alone a place where you would want to look for your food.

> "One hundred years from now, it will not matter what my bank account was, how big my house was, or what kind of car I drove. But the world may be a little better, because I was important in the life of a child."
>
> Forest Witcraft[12]

I met a group of boys who reminded me of my boys back home. I couldn't help but think of my own children having to spend their days like this—searching for food among piles of trash. As I watched the smoke rise from the piles of trash, I tried to make sense of what I was seeing and feeling.

But just a few yards away was the hope that I needed to see. World Help has been able to set up a feeding center that comes to this dump each week to feed the families and children who live nearby. They are fed a nutritious meal—one that otherwise, they would never have. And it only costs less than a dollar a day.

Osuardo is one of these children. When I met him, I asked him the same questions I had asked every child I met in Guatemala: "What is your name? How old are you?" This little boy said his name was Osuardo, but when I asked how old he was, he just turned away. I thought maybe he didn't understand me (my Spanish was rough to say the least), but when I asked again, he still did not answer. I asked an adult standing nearby, and he said Osuardo simply did not know. He did not know his birthday and therefore did not know how old he was.

If I had to guess, I would say he was about eleven or twelve years old. It really should have been no surprise that he did not know his age. His life is all about survival, and a birthday is simply a trivial thing that really does not matter in the grand scheme of things.

Osuardo is one of twelve grandchildren living with his seventy-two-year-old grandmother, Berta, in a small two-room house made of mud and straw. Berta has taken on the responsibility of raising these children after their parents died or abandoned the children. Two of her daughters live with her as well and help to take care of the children. They have no means of income and struggle to survive every day.

I wish I could accurately describe the condition of their home. It was filthy, unsanitary, and too small for a family of this size. But in the midst of the filth and smells were the beautiful, smiling faces of twelve children.

Berta pleaded with us for help. She knew the rainy season was coming, and that would mean a mess in this mud floor home. It would also mean that many of the children would become sick. With tears in her eyes, she asked for nothing for herself—she just asked us to help the children.

My friends Brenda and Tony were traveling with us and committed to providing Berta and her family with a new home for only a fraction of what we would pay here. They are now all living in a home with a kitchen, a bathroom, and more room for all the children. In addition, the children are now being sponsored and receiving an education, clothing, and food.

Earlier that day, while driving down the dusty roads of Guatemala, Brenda had asked me how you know where to help in the midst of so many great needs. She had found her answer. The needs in Guatemala and around the world are great and can be overwhelming. But there are easy and practical ways to meet those needs. We just need to be open and willing to make a difference.

How do you define poverty?

We tend to define needs by things we want, not by things we truly need to survive. We feel "poor" when we cannot afford everything we desire.[13]

The vast majority of those classified as poor in America, according to the Census Bureau, own their own car, have a VCR or DVD player, and own one or two color televisions. Forty-two percent even own their own homes. By the rest of the world's standards, this would be considered quite comfortable living.[14]

The 1.4 billion people living in extreme poverty are not just poor. They are described as living in "absolute" poverty. The United Nations defined absolute poverty as a "condition characterized by severe deprivation of human needs, including food, safe drinking water, sanitation facilities, health, shelter, education, and information."[15]

The poor always endure hardship and pain, regardless of their level of poverty or where they live. But all poverty is not the same.

I heard recently that American women are the largest consumer market and control 73 percent of household spending.[16] In my house, my husband would probably say it is more like 99 percent! And while I am picking on women, consider this: the average woman

- owns 27 pairs of shoes,
- spends 2 years of her life looking in the mirror,
- spends about 31 years of her life dieting, and
- spends about 8.5 years shopping in her lifetime.[17]

I was at a philanthropy luncheon and heard the speaker share a story about a woman who just had to have a new purse. Maybe you can relate. She was tired of her old handbags and found the perfect new one. It was just the right shade of yellow and the hot new color of the season. This bag was exactly what she had been looking for. But, it was very expensive. Even though it was far more than she wanted to pay, she convinced herself that she had to have it, purchased it, and proudly carried it home. (I like to think that maybe she snuck it home and into her house without her husband ever seeing it. Not that I have ever done that—just heard stories of women who do . . .)

> "To be without some of the things that you want is an indispensable part of happiness."
>
> Bertrand Russell[18]

A few months went by and she realized she had never carried the purse. It was actually too big and the shade of yellow really did not match anything. She never used it. It ended up just sitting on a shelf in her closet. That yellow purse became a symbol for her of all she had and all she really did not need.

We each have that yellow purse—although maybe for you it's not a purse. Maybe it's a pair of shoes, a watch, or the latest electronic gadget. It may be different for each of us, but we all have that yellow purse.

I am not suggesting we give up everything. But let's be honest—we all have things we really don't need and could easily live without.

Poverty means loss of freedom, loss of dignity, and loss of control over the fundamental course of your life. A Jamaican woman described poverty this way: "Poverty is like living in a jail, living under bondage, waiting to be free."[19]

The grip of poverty on developing countries is choking the life out of many children and their families. These are desperate people without choices. Most of us have no idea about the harsh reality of life for the children of poverty, which is that

- over one-third of children have to live in dwellings with more than five people per room;

- 134 million children have no access to any school whatsoever;
- over half a billion children have no toilet facilities whatsoever;
- almost half a billion children lack access to published information of any kind.[20]

Mother Teresa taught us, "In the poor we meet Jesus in His most distressing disguises."[21] Throughout the Bible, over two thousand verses have been found that reference the idea of the poor and alleviating poverty.[22]

Early Christians said that if a child starves to death while a Christian has extra food, then that person is guilty of murder. One of the fathers of the Church, Basil the Great, wrote in the fourth century, "When someone strips a man of his clothes, we call him a thief. And one who might clothe the naked and does not—should not he be given the same name? The bread in your cupboard belongs to the hungry; the coat in your wardrobe belongs to the naked, the shoes you let rot belong to the barefoot; the money in your vaults belongs to the destitute."[23]

But can we really end poverty? Should we even try?

If we are not careful, we will fall into the trap of thinking that helping and investing in the poor is simply a waste of time. Because the poor will "always be with us" (see Matt. 26:11), why should we even try to change things? We start to believe that no matter how hard we try, the state of the world's poor will never change. But this is simply not true. Things can change, and they already are changing. In fact, in recent years the poverty rate has dropped nearly 25 percent.[24]

At the 2000 UN Millennium Summit, 189 nations and many other international organizations agreed on eight strategic goals, known as the Millennium Development Goals, that would reduce extreme poverty by 2015:

- Eradicate Extreme Hunger and Poverty
- Achieve Universal Primary Education

- Promote Gender Equality and Empower Women
- Reduce Child Mortality
- Improve Maternal Health
- Combat HIV/AIDS, Malaria, and Other Diseases
- Ensure Environmental Sustainability
- Develop a Global Partnership for Development[25]

As you can see, the first strategic goal is to eradicate extreme hunger and poverty. One of the ways the UN plans to do this is to cut in half the number of people whose income is less than $1 a day, and progress is being made. Poverty rates dropped from 46 percent in 1990 to 27 percent in 2005. If these goals are reached by 2015 an estimated 920 million people will still be living under the international poverty line, but this is progress, and we must keep pressing forward.[26]

I am not sure that we, living our lifestyle here in the States, can relate to extreme poverty. We live a privileged life. But while that is true, it is not the main point.

In her beautiful book *The Blue Sweater*, Jacqueline Novogratz explains how she helped reconcile her lifestyle to that of the poor. After living in Rwanda for some time, one night she decided to celebrate with a friend the successes of her work so far. She had been working hard to empower people to provide for themselves and support their families. Her friend suggested they cook a fancy dinner, get dressed up, and drink some champagne.

She writes about going to a luxury store in Rwanda where many expatriates shopped. They put two bottles of champagne in their basket without even looking at the price. "At $60 each, two bottles of champagne cost more than many Rwandans earned in a year at the time." Jacqueline struggled to spend that much while living among the poor.

Her friend responded with some challenging words that are also helping me to reconcile my lifestyle with those I am trying to help. He said, "I know it doesn't make a lot of sense on one level. We're working with the really poor, and you and I couldn't be more privileged in relative terms. But don't pretend to be someone you aren't. If you were at home, you'd celebrate with champagne. If you want to remain happy and alive in this work, you need to reconcile this part of who you are and understand the inconsistencies with the work you do and how it fits into your whole way of being."

After thinking about this, Jacqueline realized that "The challenge wasn't whether to buy a couple bottles of champagne; it was instead not to take our privilege for granted and use it in a way that served the world and our highest purpose."[27]

Balakishan's father died of leprosy. His mother was suffering from the same disease and unable to care for him. So six-year-old Balakishan was living in a children's home along with hundreds of other children. I met him on my first trip to India.

Going to India is literally sensory overload. After surviving the Delhi airport, our group got on a bus to go the hotel. It was an old bus—you know the kind that has the lovely curtains on the windows. The curtains were all pulled shut. After we'd been driving for a few minutes, I decided to pull the curtain back to see what was outside. I about jumped out of my seat when I looked out and saw an elephant walking down the middle of the street! But that's India, where you never know what you will see—monkeys swinging from the trees above your head and elephants and painted cows walking down the streets.

Although these children were well taken care of, they had nothing. They slept on concrete floors, walked around without shoes, and had little access to health care and basic vaccinations.

I decided to try to find sponsors for all of the children at this home, and Balakishan would be one of the first—I would sponsor him.

I found out that he had a sister living at the home too. Her name was Mamta, and you would see her often around the home. She was always catching a ride on someone's back—not for fun but because she had no other choice. Mamta was not vaccinated as a child and had developed polio, which left her unable to walk.

She would later write her sponsor asking for a bicycle. I could not figure out what she meant. Why would she need a bicycle? She couldn't even walk. We finally realized what she was really asking for was a wheelchair. She longed for the freedom to get around on her own, without having to rely on the backs of all the other children, and to do all the things she wanted to do. The first thing she asked after receiving her new wheelchair was, "Does this mean I can go to school now?"

While working at this home, we were able to provide bunk beds for all the children who were sleeping on the hard concrete floors. What a difference that made to both their health and their dignity.

On one visit we were able to provide shoes for all of the children. After the shoes were passed out, one boy ran to a nearby field, dug a hole, and buried his shoes. He was so afraid that something would happen to them or someone would take them away that he buried his only pair of shoes.

It is easy to forget that little things can make a big difference. A bunk bed, a wheelchair, and even a pair of shoes can do a world of good in a child's life.

He was a cute and shy little boy, and meeting him was by far the highlight of my visit to Guatemala. Nine-year-old Jefferson dreams of one day becoming an architect and designing strong, magnificent buildings. But he and his four brothers and sisters are children of extreme poverty.

They live in a remote Mayan village. Like so many others in Guatemala, they live without access to clean water and other necessary resources. Most people would say that Jefferson has very little chance of realizing his dreams, but he doesn't need much to make his dreams come true. He just needs a chance to escape the cycle of poverty his family has lived in for years and years. His life is very different from mine, but in one small way, we are tied together.

A few years ago, my then nine-year-old son traveled with me to a conference. I encouraged the audience to reach out and make a difference in the life of a child through sponsorship. When I was done, I quickly made my way toward the back where our booth was located. On my way, my son stopped me and said he needed to talk. I told him it was not a good time and that it would have to wait. But he was very persistent. Something told me I needed to stop what I was doing and just listen.

I bent down in that crowded lobby and listened as my son told me something that would melt my heart. He said, "Mom, I think I want to sponsor a child." With tears in my eyes, I hugged him and realized what a special day this was.

We have always sponsored children as a family, and I have tried to impress on my children the importance of this and how they can really make a difference in someone's life. But on that day, my son had an "aha" moment and really got it for himself. He realized that he could make a difference— even at nine years old.

He picked out another little nine-year-old boy from Guatemala to sponsor. Two years later I was shaking Jefferson's hand, hugging him, and trying to explain who I was. My son had sent him a soccer ball, and his face lit up when I gave it to him. He even put up with my horrible skills and played a little soccer with me.

Meeting Jefferson was a reminder to me that the children we are trying to help are very real. They are just like our children. They have the same dreams and hopes for their lives.

It has been said, "Poverty is about hopes and dreams and how many people are prevented from dreaming."[28] I don't want Jefferson to ever have to stop dreaming.

The concept of poverty can be overwhelming, and the thought of making a difference can seem daunting. So we must narrow our focus. Instead of picturing masses of hurting people, we must begin to see the one suffering child.

When Mother Teresa was asked how she managed to rescue 50,000 people from the streets of Calcutta, she said, "I began with one."[29] Whether you grew up in the church or not, you are probably familiar with the Bible story of Sodom and Gomorrah (see Gen. 19). This city is still part of our vocabulary today; the word *sodomy* is directly related to the ancient Palestinian city of Sodom. You will still find sodomy laws all around the world. However, as familiar as we all are with these Bible stories and the use of the word today, there are some things we have overlooked.

We all know that the people of Sodom were destroyed. And we all know why, right? I believe most of us would say they were destroyed because of their immorality. However, an interesting verse in Ezekiel gives us a different perspective. It says it was because of their pride, laziness, and gluttonous lifestyle that ignored the poor and oppressed (see Ezek. 16:49 Message). Sound familiar?

Over the holidays I was doing some work in my office when my youngest son walked in. I was watching a new video that we had produced to get the word out about the need for clean water.

As I was intently watching and critiquing the video, I did not realize that my son was also watching it, but with a set of fresh, young eyes. He saw the pictures of people in desperate need and listened to how the lack of clean water affected every area of their lives.

He turned to me and said, "Mom, is that all it takes?"

I said, "Is that all it takes for what?"

He said, "Is that all it takes to give someone water—only $15?"

When I said yes, he quickly stated, "Well, I can do that!"

He had received some Christmas money and decided to give $50 toward this cause. I explained to him that his gift would provide clean water for at least three people for years to come. I could tell that he was proud of his decision—he knew he had made a good investment.

I've heard it said, "We can be the most generous people we know, just with what we have."

So I think I finally know the answer to that question: "What would the reward be for the person who knows the meaning of enough?" I think the person who knows the meaning of enough is rewarded by the feeling you get when you can finally ask a new question: "Is that all it takes to make a difference?"

5

I Knew You Would Come

My song is love
Love to the loveless shown
And it goes on
You don't have to be alone

Coldplay[1]

By the time we arrived to visit my grandfather, hospice was taking care of him, and they had moved him to a special bed on the main level of his home. My sister and I walked in the back door and immediately saw him lying almost lifeless in his bed. I quickly ran over to him and leaned over so he could see me. He was pale and having trouble breathing. The cancer had taken over his body, and he was barely clinging to life.

He looked up and said the words I will never forget: "I knew you would come."

My grandfather was a coal miner from West Virginia. He was a simple, quiet man. He and my grandmother were the one constant in my young life. When I was growing up, my parents were part of a "revival" ministry, and we traveled all the time in an Airstream trailer, living on church parking lots. My husband likes to say that I grew up in the circus. He has a point. But that part of my life is a complete story in and of itself.

For a little girl who had no real place to call home, my grandparents' house became home to me—the place I loved to go and never wanted to leave. They lived a simple and quiet life so different from my own. At their house I found peace and unconditional love.

Their home was near downtown Huntington, West Virginia, just blocks away from Marshall University. They knew all of their neighbors and had known them for years. The street their house was on was so old that it was actually made of bricks. The rumbling of the bricks underneath the tires of our car was one of my favorite parts of the journey and what told me we were close. Even before I was big enough to really see out of the car and where we were going, this sound told me I was home. When we heard it my siblings and I would all start singing "Follow the Yellow Brick Road."

It is funny what things you remember about your childhood. I don't really remember the big monumental things but instead remember the small, almost insignificant details. But it seems that it is these details all mushed together that really make us the people we become.

My grandfather was always humming a happy, carefree tune. Whether he was cooking or working in his shed, you could hear a sweet song. He was an amazing cook, and he always made us the most incredible pancakes for breakfast. He could also peel an entire apple with one seamless spiral peel using his pocket knife. It was one of my favorite things to watch him do.

Memories come flooding back when you are looking at someone reaching the end of their life. My grandfather had given me some wonderful memories, and in his last days he gave me one more. It was as if he had been waiting for us, as if he was holding on until my sister and I arrived so that we could say our good-byes. He gave me a priceless gift that day: a chance to look my beloved grandfather in the eyes, tell him that I loved him, and in my heart, tell him good-bye.

He died just days later, and I soon realized that those special words he said to me were some of the last words of his life: "I knew you would come."

As a child, I thought of my dad as an adventurer—Indiana Jones or Jacques Cousteau! He traveled around the world and brought me treasures from every location—wood carvings of giraffes, bracelets made out of zebra tails, and the stacking Russian matryoshka dolls.

I listened to him tell the stories of his travels to Eastern Europe and Romania. I heard of the great persecution the believers there faced during those difficult times. He told me stories of smuggling Bibles in, meeting in secret, and armed soldiers standing guard at each church service. He was detained at the border many times, sometimes for hours, and followed by the secret service.

He told me about a church that the government wanted to knock down. The night before it was scheduled for demolition, the church members locked themselves in the building and prayed all night. The next morning, the soldiers left and the building was saved.

The story I remember most was about my dad's close Romanian pastor friend. During the years of communism, his wife was diagnosed with cancer. The bone marrow transplant surgery that she needed was only available in England. When she went to apply for her visa, the government officials said they would give it to her if she would do one simple thing— renounce her faith in Christ. Without hesitating, she said she could not do that and walked out of their office. Within two months, she died.

I was astonished by that kind of deep faith.

When I was a little older I was able to travel to Romania and experience it for myself. I saw firsthand the difficulties they faced every day just to follow Christ. I fell in love with the Romanian people and especially their children.

These were the years when the Romanian orphanage system was all over our news. ABC's *20/20* even did a report on it in 1990 showing one orphanage where "babies were stacked on the shelves of a cart like loaves of bread."[2] Ceausescu's plan to force women to have at least five children had resulted in a crisis of overcrowded children's homes and overworked child care providers.

> "God is in the slums, in the cardboard boxes where the poor play house. God is in the silence of a mother who has infected her child with a virus that will end both their lives. God is in the cries heard under the rubble of war. God is in the debris of wasted opportunity and lives, and God is with us if we are with them."
>
> Bono[3]

The conditions in these institutions were deplorable. I know—I saw some of it for myself. Reports were showing the inhumane treatment of these children. But what I also saw was not a lack of caring from the workers but simply too few workers. There were just not enough people to care for all the children.

I remember walking through one of these institutions and into a room where many of the toddlers were staying. We were instructed not to hold them or pick them up. My heart nearly broke in two as I had to walk through that room looking down on all of those children raising their arms up to me, just begging to be held and loved. World Help's child sponsorship program began by helping many of these Romanian children.

I recently returned to Romania with my dad to celebrate the one hundredth anniversary of our partnering church—the one that had almost been bulldozed down years before.

It also was the anniversary of the week that the revolution started twenty years earlier.

Romania has changed much over the years. There are now shopping malls and McDonald's restaurants. But the average person still has trouble making ends meet. A doctor barely makes $500 a month, and eating at McDonalds is a luxury for most people.

Some of the first children we sponsored were Ana, Bianca, Marius, and John. I still keep in touch with them today and was able to see some of them on this trip. I first met them when they were just in grade school, and now they are grown adults. In some ways they are still struggling to find their place in the world and in a country whose economy and systems are not making it easy on them. But they were given a chance when so many children in their country were simply thrown away.

José was less than a year old when he was abandoned by his alcoholic parents. He was alone for two days before he was found in a remote village of Guatemala. His mother had left him outside in these terrible conditions for three days without food or water. José's mother was mentally unstable and had already caused his brother's death through neglect.

In addition, José was very sick. The dirty water and lack of food had caught up with this small infant. Between the sickness and his mother's neglect, José seemed destined to die before his first birthday. But God had other plans for this special little boy. He was rescued by Carlos, our partner in Guatemala. This kind man provided him with medical care and slowly nursed him back to health.

José was given a second chance at life. He was given clean water, food, shelter, and lots of love. He was also given an education and a chance for a future.

Twenty years later, José is now attending a university. His education is giving him knowledge and an incredible opportunity—a chance to give back. Every week, José hikes up into the hills to rescue dying children. He sees himself in the face of every child he helps and knows what it will take to change their lives: clean water and an education.

José knows that in order to keep the children from becoming ill, their families must have access to safe water. He knows that until the children stop getting sick, they will not be able to attend school. And until they can attend school, they will never have the opportunities they need to follow their dreams.

> "When a poor person dies of hunger, it has not happened because God did not take care of him or her. It has happened because neither you nor I wanted to give that person what he or she needed."
>
> Mother Teresa[4]

Two-thirds of children growing up in Guatemala live in poverty, and chronic malnutrition affects 80 percent of indigenous children. "Nearly three million Guatemalans lack access to safe water, and 6 million have no access to improved sanitation."[5] These conditions create an environment that is not friendly to children and makes it nearly impossible for them to survive their own childhoods.

When I met Lex, he was so full of life and all boy! All he wanted to do was throw a ball. He would throw it on the ground, I would pick it up and hand it back to him, and he would throw it down again, over and over and over again. I think he could have done that all day. This little boy from Guatemala, who was only about a year old, absolutely captured my heart forever.

Lex is one of the lucky children in Guatemala. He is being cared for by Hope of Life's Baby Rescue Center. He is blessed, because there are thousands and thousands of other children just like Lex who are not so lucky. They live in hunger and pain every day of their lives, and many of them don't survive.

I had so much fun playing with Lex. His love of throwing balls reminded me of my son Bentley, who also always has a ball in his hand. It's funny how you see your own children in the eyes of others. I have seen my children all around the world.

But as happy and healthy as Lex looked to me, there was a tragic story behind his beautiful eyes. When Lex was only a few days old, he became very ill. His mother had other children to care for and no way to really provide for them all. It is unclear whether she was abusive, neglectful, or just at her wit's end. But whatever the reason—she just snapped. She decided she could not handle a sick and crying baby anymore.

She wrapped Lex in a blanket and took him outside, where she proceeded to dig a hole. She laid him in the hole, and while he was still breathing, she covered his body with dirt. She literally buried him alive.

As I held this handsome and happy little boy in my arms, I could not believe what I was hearing as I was told his story, and even now, I am having trouble recounting it. As a mother, I could not imagine how his mother could do this. It was unbelievable. Thankfully, this was not the end of Lex's story.

A thirteen-year-old girl living in the same village saw Lex's mother commit this horrible crime. She just knew something was wrong. She went and got her uncle to help. Together they dug Lex out of that hole, and amazingly, he survived! That is how he ended up at the Baby Rescue Center, where he was nursed back to health.

Lex is truly a miracle baby—and I was holding him in my arms. He had already stolen my heart, and after hearing his story, I knew I would never get it back.

A couple hundred dollars can save a child like Lex. That's pocket change for us here in America. It doesn't take much to show up in a child's life and be their hero.

But for every child like José and Lex, to whom help comes, there are others for whom help just doesn't make it in time.

They heard help was coming, so they traveled from miles and miles away with the hope that their children could somehow be saved.

The small, almost forgotten village of Chinacadenas, Guatemala, is home to hundreds of Mayan Indians. A civil war that only recently ended has devastated their villages and culture. Many children have become orphans. Malnutrition is rampant. Sickness and disease are a daily part of life. Their stories are heartbreaking.

Over the years, my mom has traveled with my dad all over the world and seen her fair share of need, poverty, and despair. But one of her first comments to me was that she had never seen poverty like she saw in Guatemala—not in Africa, India, or anywhere else. She was amazed at what she saw and experienced.

Three families had heard that our group was coming to this village and traveled hours to bring their sick and dying children. Each one held a tiny infant on the verge of death. All were severely malnourished and suffering from waterborne illnesses. One had a cleft palate, and one was so badly infected with worms that they were literally crawling out of her mouth and ears. Can you imagine?

But this was a special day. This was the day that three babies were rescued. This was the day that three lives were forever changed.

This was the day that hope arrived.

The babies were taken to the Baby Rescue Center, where children's lives are saved every day. My mom and the other ladies in our group got to spend the day working with the children in the center, feeding them, cleaning them, playing with them, and just loving them. One of our ladies was so touched by what she saw that she offered to pay for the surgery to repair the girl's cleft palate. That little girl's life will never be the same.

I truly believe that if we want to change our world and really make a difference, there is no better place to start than in the life of a child.

We overuse the word *compassion*. Both people of faith and the secular world use this word, but do we comprehend the true meaning? I really can't think of a more beautiful word. But do we really understand it?

Compassion is not pity. It is not simply feeling sorry for someone. It is not sadness or an emotion that we feel.

Most dictionaries define compassion as the awareness of need and the wish to alleviate it. I would take it a step further. True compassion—the compassion that Jesus had in the Bible when he was "moved with compassion" (Mark 1:41 NASB)—is more than awareness and a wish. This kind of compassion requires movement, advocacy, and action.

When we read that Jesus was "moved with compassion," it is always when he was confronted with great human need. And when he was confronted, he always responded with action. He touched the need. When he healed the blind, the lame, and the leper, he literally and physically touched them.

Pity sees and even feels, but compassion touches the need. True compassion requires two important things—action and touching. I couldn't agree more with the following thoughts from Henri Nouwen:

> This is what compassion means. It is not a bending toward the under-privileged from a privileged position; it is not a reaching out from on high to those who are less fortunate below; it is not a gesture of sympathy or pity for those who fail to make it in the upward pull. On the contrary, compassion means going directly to those people and places where suffering is most acute and building a home there. . . . It is the compassion of God who does not merely act as a servant, but who expresses the divinity of God through servanthood.[6]

Over the years, I have thought about my grandfather's last words to me, "I knew you would come." Those words have made me think of something bigger than myself and my family. They have made me think of the children.

Children around the world are waiting. They are waiting for someone to rescue them from hunger, disease, sickness, abuse, and slavery. They long to say, "I knew you would come." But unless we respond, for many children, we are simply too late. No one comes to rescue them—there is no hero.

Next month I will return to Guatemala to go on a baby rescue mission. We will hike into the hills and reach children that help and hope usually do not travel as far to find. We want to document on video the stories of these children who are suffering from the effects of malnutrition and unclean water. I hope and pray that through our telling their stories, people will see how together we can make a difference and literally save lives.

The sad part about this trip is that we don't have to worry about whether there will be children to rescue when we go. They are always there and always waiting.

I am trying to prepare myself for what I know I will see. Some of these children will be too sick by the time we arrive. All we will be able to do is help their families bury them. Some may die en route to the hospital, just steps away from help. But for others, we will be just in time. When I hold that special child in my arms—the one who may not have survived unless we came—I know I will hear those words whispered once again in my ear: *I knew you would come.*

6

The Ripple Effect

*There is no tool for development more
effective than the empowerment of women.*

Kofi Annan[1]

We were all standing in the crowded foyer of the church, right outside the main sanctuary. It was the holidays and this was a special "Hanging of the Greens" service to both decorate the church and focus on the true meaning of Christmas. Families volunteered to carry in different things—wreaths, garland, poinsettias—and in between the pastor would read a passage from the Christmas story.

My family and I were waiting in the back for our turn, along with all of the other families, and listening to the pastor read from Luke 1: "God sent the angel Gabriel to Nazareth, a town in Galilee, to a virgin pledged to be married to a man named Joseph, a descendant of David. The virgin's name was Mary" (vv. 26–27).

75

My son was about three at the time, and when he heard those words, he looked up at me and said loudly enough for everyone in the room to hear, "Mom, you used to be a virgin." The room seemed to go silent, and all eyes were on me. I was humiliated and embarrassed but laughing a little too. I knew what he really meant was that I used to not have children, but no one else was really hearing what I was hearing. I have to admit it was pretty funny, and years later, we are still laughing.

"What would men be without women? Scarce, sir, mighty scarce."

Mark Twain[2]

But there is nothing funny about the way a young girl's virginity is being used in many places today. Either her virginity or her lack of it can lead to deadly consequences all around the world.

In a remote region of India lives an almost forgotten community. In the Indian caste system, this community is one of the lowest. The people are extremely poor and lack economic and developmental opportunities. Their lifestyle and beliefs should be dark secrets, but they live them openly for all to see and no one to stop.

For the past five hundred years, they have been using prostitution as their primary source of income. The firstborn daughter of every family is placed into prostitution at the very young age of twelve. What makes this even more shocking is that the parents and brothers initiate this, and the entire community lives off the earnings.

Since this is socially accepted, the girls enter their new profession through a special ceremony. Following this ceremony, wealthy men pay a lot of money to have sexual relations with one of the young virgin girls. Many of these girls are eventually sold into prostitution rings throughout Western Asia.

One of these girls named Neetu told one of our partners, "I knew what was in store for me when I was five years old. My mother told me and also I have seen other girls going through the same ceremony. So I have accepted this life."

Her mother said, "I wanted to make her look pretty. Why shouldn't I do it? My mother did for my elder sister when she turned twelve years old. Now it is my turn because Neetu is the oldest among my three daughters. It is my duty to get her prepared for her new life."

Can you imagine sending your daughter off into this kind of life? Or your sister, niece, or cousin? If you are a young girl yourself, can you imagine knowing this will be your life and having no choice?

It is impossible to wake up to the world without addressing the issue of women and girls, for this issue affects every other issue facing the world today. As Jessica Laufer has said, "Investing in the education and empowerment of girls and women has a ripple effect of positive change—it has been shown to decrease HIV/AIDS rates, increase GDP, decrease infant, child and maternal mortality, and increase civic participation."[3]

In fact, with only a few years left to reach the Millennium Development Goals, it has been said that "discrimination and inequality [of women] are holding back progress on all of the Goals, which include gender equality and women's empowerment, reducing hunger and poverty, achieving universal primary education, improving maternal health and combating HIV and AIDS."[4]

I believe that if you want to truly change the world today, this is one issue and cause you simply cannot ignore. But it is also impossible to address all the issues facing women and girls around the world today in one chapter. So let me attempt to summarize and give you a broad overview of what women and girls are up against today.

Poverty

Six hundred million girls live in the developing world.[5] Women make up an estimated 70 percent of people living in extreme poverty.[6] A young girl living in poverty in the developing world faces a life with little or no education, a forced child marriage or the possibility of being sold into slavery or sex trafficking, a high risk of HIV infection, and a high risk of an early pregnancy that could take her life. All of this carries her down into a pit so deep that it is almost impossible to ever climb back out.

HIV/AIDS

AIDS is the largest public health problem the world has ever faced. It has already surpassed the bubonic plague, which wiped out 25 million people.[7] An estimated 30 million people worldwide have died from AIDS.[8] Studies show that women and especially young women are more susceptible to HIV infection than men. Of the 42 million people still living with HIV/AIDS, 70 percent are in sub-Saharan Africa.[9] And in Africa, 75 percent of those infected are female.[10]

More and more women who are of child-bearing age have HIV through no fault of their own, due in large part to rape or husbands who are infected. Mothers are passing the disease to their unborn children. These children can be infected before they ever enter the world. Millions of children have been orphaned or left to care for their dying parents or siblings.

Rape

Rape has been and is still being used around the world as a genocidal weapon and a tool in war to bring suffering and even death. During the Rwandan genocide, soldiers were instructed to rape the women, knowing they would infect them with HIV.

In Sierra Leone, "Violence against women was not just incidental to the conflict, but was routinely used as a tool of war. Sexual violence was used in a widespread and systematic way as a weapon, and women were raped in extraordinarily brutal ways." It has been estimated that over half of the women there have "endured sexual violence or the threat of it during the upheavals in that country."[11] The UN estimates that as many as "90 percent of girls and women over the age of three were sexually abused in parts of Liberia during the civil war there."[12]

Even when war or genocide is not the reason for conflict, rape can be used in a way that seems almost more cruel, if that is even possible. In countries obsessed with a woman's virginity, rape is used to prey on the poor and uneducated. Families are shamed, and young girls are left with a choice to take their own lives or move their entire families to avoid the embarrassment and harassment from their communities. The police and authorities are no help and simply go along with a culture that gives women in these situations no rights.

The World Bank did a study on ten selected risk factors facing girls and women ages fifteen to forty-four. They found "rape and domestic violence more dangerous than cancer, motor vehicle accidents, war and malaria."[13]

Gender Discrimination

It is estimated that 60 to 100 million females are missing from the globe today, because "Every year at least another 2 million girls worldwide disappear because of gender discrimination."[14] These lives are cut short only because they were women. Gender discrimination is the basis for many of the issues facing women today, and until we address it, women will continue to "perform two-thirds of the world's work, [but] only earn one tenth of the income, and own less than one percent of the world's property."[15] This leaves women vulnerable and at risk.

In addition, young girls are being abused around the world, whether from selective abortion or simply neglecting them after birth by not vaccinating them or taking them to the hospital when sick. Many girls are ignored, not given the food and medicine they need to survive; baby girls are aborted, and young girls are sold into slavery and often prostitution. "It appears that more girls have been killed in the last fifty years, precisely because they were girls, than men were killed in all the wars of the twentieth century. More girls are killed in this routine 'gendercide' in any one decade than people were slaughtered in all the genocides of the twentieth century."[16]

Trafficking

It is estimated that 600,000 to 800,000 people are trafficked each year. The majority—an estimated 80 percent—are women and girls.[17] Not surprising is the fact that the majority of these women come from the poorest places in the world, where it is easier to prey on innocent victims.

Trafficking has become a 32-billion-dollar industry, so successful that groups are switching from drugs and other illegal products to human beings. It has been found to produce a "higher profit and lower risk."[18] Hard to believe, but true.

While most trafficking victims are forced into prostitution and sexual exploitation, they can also be forced into begging, the military, marriage, slavery, or even illegal adoption.

Human trafficking is occurring all around the world—even in the United States. But in the country of Nepal alone, rural girls are routinely trafficked into India so that young Indian men can mess around until they get married and nice middle-class Indian young women can keep their purity. While 200,000 Nepali women and girls are already in Indian brothels, an additional 5,000 to 7,000 are trafficked every year. After being locked up for days, denied food, raped, and beaten, they can be expected to service up to twenty-five clients per day.[19]

It is estimated that in the United States, 100,000 to 300,000 children are in slavery and being used for sexual exploitation. Yet our government "spends 300 times more money per year to fight drug trafficking than it does to fight human trafficking."[20]

Maternal Health

"One in three girls in the developing world is married before she is eighteen and one in seven marries by fifteen. At this rate 100 million girls will become child brides over the next decade."[21] The ramifications of this are great, but one of the greatest effects is on a young girl's health. For girls ages fifteen to nineteen, pregnancy and childbirth is the leading cause of death in the developing world.[22]

Every year, 500,000 women die from childbirth. That is one woman every minute.[23] A woman in sub-Saharan Africa has a 1 in 22 chance of dying during labor.[24] "In addition to deaths, over 300 million women worldwide suffer long-term health problems and disability arising from complications from pregnancy or delivery."[25]

One of the major maternal complications facing many women today is obstetric fistulas. This condition is basically a hole in the birth canal produced by a long and obstructed labor. A woman can literally be left with a hole that extends from the vagina to the rectum. Surgeries can repair up to 90 percent of these conditions, but most of these women lack proper medical attention or have no access to it, so they don't have a chance.[26] Women are left with no control of their bladder and bowels, meaning there can be a constant flow of urine and feces. The smell can be unbearable, making social interaction nearly impossible. In addition, nerve damage can also leave some unable to walk. Young girls are even more prone to this condition since their bodies are still developing. I know this is not a pleasant thing to talk about, but imagine if you were one of the 2 million women around the world suffering from this humiliating condition.[27]

Out of all the Millennium Development Goals, maternal health is considered to be the most "off-track."[28]

Education

There is a saying in Ghana that "if you educate a man, you simply educate an individual, but if you educate a woman, you educate a nation."[29] It has been proven that an educated girl is more likely to stay healthy, get a job, and marry later. And all of this has the power to change her life and the life of her community.

But most girls in the developing world are never given a chance to change their own life.

Out of all the illiterate adults in the world, two-thirds are women[30]—or 600 million women as compared to 320 million men.[31] There are 130 million kids out of school around the world, and 70 percent are girls—70 percent![32]

Studies show that in sub-Saharan Africa and many other areas around the world, women and young girls must walk an average of four miles every day just to provide water for their families.[33] The consequences are tragic. Young girls have no time for school, and women have little time to pursue economic opportunities that would financially benefit their families. The long-term damage and ripple effects of this loss of time are too great to measure.

But lack of water is not the only thing that keeps girls out of school. Early marriage deters many, as their parents and culture perceive that school is a waste of time. For instance, in a region of Ethiopia, "one in every three girls who were not in school said that the primary reason was marriage."[34] Distance to school and the danger in getting there are also factors that prevent girls from getting an education.

The lack of education for women is literally costing lives. It is estimated that 1.8 million deaths could have been prevented in sub-Saharan Africa alone. The reason is that women with a secondary education are more likely to be aware of the drugs that can be used to reduce the spread of HIV from mother to child. For instance, "in Malawi, 60 percent of mothers with secondary education or higher were aware that drugs could reduce transmission risks, compared with 27 percent of women with no education."[36]

> "We have to free half of the human race, the women, so that they can help to free the other half."
>
> Emmeline Pankhurst[35]

The UN Secretary-General said, "Investing in girls and women is likely to prevent inter-generational cycles of poverty and yield high economic and societal returns."[37]

If you educate a girl she will

- earn up to 25 percent more and reinvest 90 percent in her family;
- be three times less likely to become HIV positive; and
- have fewer, healthier children who are 40 percent more likely to live past the age of five.[38]

A girl's income can increase by 10 to 20 percent with simply one extra year of education.[39] As Nelson Mandela once said, "Education is the most powerful weapon which you can use to change the world."[40] And it has been found that when the participation of women in the labor force has increased, poverty rates have declined.[41] In contrast, in places where fewer girls are educated, human development rates are low.[42]

In Kenya, the Nike Foundation did a study that concluded that adolescent pregnancies were costing the Kenyan economy $500 million per year. By simply investing more in girls, Kenya could add $3.2 billion to their economy.[43]

To me, it just makes sense to invest in girls.

As startling as these statistics are, we hear very little about them on the evening news. In their groundbreaking and eye-opening book *Half the Sky*, journalists Nicholas Kristof and Sheryl WuDunn talk about the unfair and unbalanced attitude toward women:

> We came across an obscure but meticulous demographic study that outlined a human rights violation that had claimed tens of thousands more lives. This study found that thirty-nine thousand baby girls die annually in China because parents don't give them the same medical care and attention that boys receive—and that is just in the first year of life. . . . Those Chinese girls never received a column inch of news coverage, and we began to wonder if our journalistic priorities were skewed. . . .
>
> When a prominent dissident was arrested in China, we would write a front-page article; when 100,000 girls were routinely kidnapped and trafficked into brothels, we didn't even consider it news. Partly that is because we journalists tend to be good at covering events that happen on a particular day, but we slip at covering events that happen every day—such as the quotidian cruelties inflicted on women and girls. We journalists weren't the only ones who dropped the ball on this subject: Less than 1 percent of U.S. foreign aid is specifically targeted to women and girls.[44]

When I think about the people I have met around the world, the stories that have touched me the most are the stories of young girls and women. Perhaps it is because so many women are suffering, or perhaps it is because as a woman, I instinctively care about this issue. But men should not ignore it. In fact, men are needed more than ever—men who are strong, brave, and willing to break down the walls of injustice. As David Palmer said, "Maybe the kingdom of God needs a few more who are willing to kick some tail and take names if necessary. Sure, we need to pray for victims of injustice, but has anyone thought of, well, like, *rescuing* them? My afterlife view of justice is real convenient since neither I nor my daughter is the one being beaten senseless with electrical cords."[45]

Esther was just over six years old when her mom first abandoned her. The woman left the confused little girl and her sister with an aunt in a rural area of South Africa and then disappeared for a year. The child lost much more than her mother during that time. Esther and her sister were repeatedly raped and molested by family members. Like all children who are sexually abused, Esther was haunted for years by the shame and painful memories.

By the age of nine, Esther had already contemplated suicide to escape her horrible life. But the thought of leaving her younger sister kept her from following through.

When her mother returned, they began living with cousins. Again the young girls were molested. Their mother moved them to live with other distant relatives, and once again she disappeared. Esther started to go to school even though she began to realize that no one cared if she did or not. Still she kept on.

To raise money for books, school supplies, and something to wear to school, Esther gleaned corn from fields. She gathered all the corn left behind during the harvest and sold it to a shop owner. But instead of money for the corn she had harvested, Esther would beg for books, a pencil or material to make school clothes.

After seven long years, Esther's mother showed up again and moved them to a boarding school. Esther felt as if she were simply being dumped. There was still no money and her mother rarely visited. But to Esther this new home was heaven. She was receiving three meals a day, and all she had to do was obey and study. To her, this was a dream. But when her mother could no longer pay the boarding fees, they were forced to leave.

Esther survived her difficult childhood and has turned her pain into a way to help abandoned and needy children. When I sat down with the then fifty-seven-year-old woman at her home, she was joyful and gracious but determined to get help for her children.

She told me that at the time approximately 260 babies were abandoned every month in South Africa. They were left at police stations, at children's homes, at hospitals, in fields, and in trash cans. Esther was taking in many of these children no one else wanted. She told me that they need education, clothing, love, and moral support—the very things she so desperately needed growing up.

In Gulu, northern Uganda, I met with a most remarkable group of about twenty mothers. They are all HIV positive and have been abandoned by their husbands, left to raise their children alone. Unfortunately, this story is common across sub-Saharan Africa. Innocent women are infected with a deadly disease by the men who are supposed to love them and care for them. And if that blow is not big enough, they either quickly become widows, or they are abandoned.

What was so inspirational about these women was their sheer determination. They have not given up on life. They have not lost hope. They are pushing forward together to build a future for their children. All of the women volunteer at a local center that helps to feed needy and orphaned children. They labor over hot cooking fires to feed hundreds of hungry little mouths. They also work together in a small co-op, working in a garden to grow fresh vegetables to feed their families as well as to sell to provide an income.

One thirty-six-year-old mother named Kristine shared her story. "I was married when I was twenty, and so far, I have five children. The day I found out I had the disease, I thought,

'This is the end of me.' I wanted to commit suicide, because I thought that I would die at any moment anyway."

Kristine said that during this dark period in her life, she heard about Jesus for the first time. "I accepted Christ as my personal Savior. Since then, my life has changed."

Because the young mother received some help and vocational training, she said, "Now I am tailoring, baking, and making dye. I told them about my sickness and they began to support my family. They sponsored some of my children into the program so that they could have food and schooling. I really appreciate the work of these people. They taught me about the Lord. Now I know that the Lord I am serving is the One that made the blind to see and the lame to walk. I know that he can touch me."

Shannon Galpin of the nonprofit Mountain2Mountain says,

The time of turning a blind eye, of ignoring the headlines, or saying, "but what can I do about it?" has passed. The time for change is now. No longer can we ignore the women raped around the world, the girls trafficked across borders for prostitution, or the unplanned babies born to both. No more can we dismiss genital mutilation, ironing breasts, or other torturous concepts that put the blame of rape and childhood pregnancy on the women, instead of punishing the men that perpetrate the crimes. Mutilating women to stem sexual assault just adds insult to injury. It is not acceptable that as women living in the West, enjoying freedoms women before us fought for, that we do not rally, advocate, and work to ensure that women EVERY-WHERE have these freedoms. It is not enough to shout against the injustice done to women across the globe. Action is the key.[46]

Back in that remote village of India, the lives of Indian girls are starting to change. Through World Help's child sponsorship program as well as a community outreach program, these people are being introduced to a new way of life that they have never known. Our goal is to educate them so they don't have to buy into the cultural lifestyle of prostitution. Hundreds of children and especially young girls are being helped through these programs.

Robert Kennedy once said, "Each time a man stands up for an ideal, or acts to improve the lot of others, or strikes out against an injustice, he sends forth a tiny ripple of hope."[47] I believe if we send out a ripple of hope for women and girls around the world, we will see it return tenfold. We will see a ripple effect that really can change the world.

7

Crystal Clear

Water is the sleeping giant issue of the twenty-first century and we all need to wake up about it.

Robert Redford[1]

I drove down my driveway and pulled up in front of my house, not noticing that half my yard was under water. It had been a long day, and I was looking forward to cooking dinner and spending the evening with my family. My husband arrived home a few minutes after I did and, of course, immediately noticed the flood in our front yard. We quickly realized that we had a water line break and had to immediately shut off the water to our house.

In one moment, my life came to a screeching halt. I couldn't cook dinner, my kids could not use the bathroom, they couldn't take a bath—nothing. We had no choice but to pack up and stay with my in-laws until our water problem could be fixed.

I would like to say that I had a good attitude about all of this . . . but I didn't. I was so upset that my plans had been ruined and that I had been inconvenienced. After pouting and making my husband miserable for most of the evening, it hit me. I was in the middle of a huge new project that had me researching the incredible need for water around the world. I had just experienced a very, very small taste of what people experience around the world every day, and I had failed miserably.

Antonia lives in an area of Guatemala known as Chiquimula. I'm told it has the highest rate of infant mortality in all of Guatemala. There are over three hundred families in her village, and each one is struggling to survive.

Our Guatemalan partner is a regular fixture there. Through our help, he is able to take them food and medicine. However, this village still needs clean water.

He has rescued many children from Chiquimula who have been close to death. In fact, he rescues thousands of children from the most remote parts of Guatemala and brings them to his Baby Rescue Center. There children receive medical care, food, clean water, and love.

His greatest struggle is not in saving them but in keeping the ones he has saved healthy. He knows some of the children he returns home will become sick and need rescuing once again.

Little Antonia had a brother, but our partner could not save him in time. However, he was able to help Antonia's sister. She underwent an amazing recovery at the center, and when better, she was taken back to her parents.

At the time, Antonia wasn't sick, but within a few months she needed urgent medical care herself. When our partner went back to the village, he found her sister had become ill again and died. Although Antonia is now healthy, without the clean water she needs, our partner will be returning to rescue her time and time again.

If asked why these children keep getting sick, he would say just one word: *water*. They have food, medicine, clothing, and shelter. The only thing they don't have is clean water, and it's killing them. They are dying from waterborne diseases.

Eighty-six percent of all urban waste-water in Latin America is discharged untreated into rivers, lakes, and oceans.[2] Contaminated water is bringing disease and death.

> "We forget that the water cycle and the life cycle are one."
> Jacques Cousteau[3]

I told you in the last chapter that if you really want to wake up to the world, you cannot ignore the issue of women. But equally important is the issue of clean water, for it too can have a ripple effect that impacts every area of life—health, economy, and education.

Kofi Annan, the former UN Secretary-General, said, "We shall not finally defeat AIDS, tuberculosis, malaria, or any of the other infectious diseases that plague the developing world until we have also won the battle for safe drinking water, sanitation and basic health care."[4]

The World Bank reports, "Water is crucial to human life. It is important not only for the everyday needs of drinking, washing, and cleaning, but also for growing crops to feed the population, for generating power to provide electricity, and for maintaining ecosystems such as wetlands. It plays a vital role in people's livelihoods, economic growth, and the well-being of all species."[5]

It is estimated that nearly 5 percent of the gross domestic product (GDP) of African countries is lost due to the sickness and disease caused by unclean water.[6] The absence of an adequate supply of water makes it nearly impossible to grow crops, which provide income for families and communities. Without clean water, people are sick and can't work or attend school. And without clean, safe water, poverty never goes away.

A crucial part of the Millennium Development Goals is to cut in half the number of people who lack access to clean and safe water.[7] Our world leaders know that one of the best ways to help end poverty is by providing clean water. But despite their power and influence, they will never reach their goals alone. We must all buy into this, and we are all part of the solution. And as important as the Millennium Development Goals are, it is estimated that even if these goals are met by 2015, there will still be 800 million people without access to clean water and over 1.8 billion people without basic sanitation.[8]

Unclean water, together with the poor sanitation it creates, is the number one killer in the entire world.[9] Combine war, malaria, HIV/AIDS, and even traffic accidents—lack of clean water still kills more people.[10]

"About 29,000 children under the age of 5—21 each minute—die every day, mainly from preventable causes," reports UNICEF. "Malnutrition and the lack of safe water and sanitation contribute to half of all these children's deaths."[11]

A single sip of water is all it takes to be infected. A single drop of water can contain over 1 billion bacterial organisms.[12] The following is only a partial list of water-related diseases.

Diarrhea

Each year, 2.2 million deaths occur due to diarrhea brought about through dirty water.[13] Five thousand children will die today from it.[14] One of the effects of diarrhea is dehydration. When a child begins to suffer dehydration, the only option for him or her is more dirty water. This is a death sentence for millions of children.

One very important aspect of diarrhea is the direct link to malnutrition. Diarrhea causes food to not be properly digested and stored by the body. Even if it does not result in death, it can lead to "stunting of growth, intellectual impairment, and diminished productive and creative capacities."[15]

Malaria

The CDC reports that "3.3 billion people (half the world's population) live in areas at risk of malaria transmission."[16] Each year 1.3 million people die of malaria, and 90 percent of them are children.[17] Transmission rates are dramatically increased due to unmanaged water sources. These stagnant water sources are a breeding ground for mosquitoes which transmit malaria.[18]

Trachoma

An unbelievable 500 million people are at risk for this disease which leads to blindness, and 128 million of these cases are children. There is a strong correlation between trachoma and a lack of face washing, most often due to the absence of nearby clean water sources.[19] The vast majority of these cases lie in sub-Saharan Africa. In Uganda, close to 40 percent of all children are affected by trachoma.[20]

Worms and Parasites

Simply being infected by worms and parasites can lead to cognitive impairment, massive dysentery, or anemia. These are conditions children may not die from but which severely lessen their opportunity to attend school. Worms also interfere with the digestion and absorption of food. Children with worms suffer from bloated stomachs, pain, and diarrhea.[21]

Typhoid

Typhoid fever is the result of bacteria ingested by eating contaminated foods and, most commonly, drinking unclean water. According to the World Health Organization, there are as many as 33 million cases and 600,000 deaths from typhoid fever annually.[22] In some countries, 90 percent of typhoid cases are children ages three to nineteen.[23]

Cholera

Cholera is a substantial health burden in many countries in Africa, Asia, and South and Central America, where it is endemic. Cholera is an intestinal infection contracted through contaminated water as well as food. Ninety-four percent of all reported cases occur in Africa. A recent estimate puts the number of people who die from cholera each year at about 120,000 and the total number of yearly cholera cases worldwide at 3 to 5 million.[24] Even if clean water is trucked in during an outbreak, it is often not enough.[25] We saw this most recently in Haiti after the 2010 earthquake. Over 300,000 became sick due to cholera and at least 5,000 died.[26]

Numbers in Perspective

I don't like to simply focus on numbers, because each of these numbers represents a life and a story. Numbers can also too easily seem overwhelming. But some numbers are helpful— the numbers that show how easy it is to make a difference.

The worldwide water crisis could be solved with 20 to 30 billion dollars a year.[27] Yet Americans spend $16 billion each year on bottled water alone.

Americans also spend an average of $700 each at Christmas,[28] which, with a population of a little over 300 million, works out to over $210 billion. Even if we take the high estimate of $30 billion, if just half the population set aside $200 of their Christmas spending and put it toward the water crisis, the problem could be solved!

Sometimes numbers make a lot of sense.

Did you flush your toilet today? Just once? You have already used more water than the average African has for an entire day—for drinking, cooking, cleaning, bathing, washing . . . everything. Just one flush.[29]

Most of us have no idea what it is really like to be without water. Today I am looking out onto a big beautiful lake. Summer is here. Boats are buzzing by, children are jumping in and swimming, people are fishing, and everyone is having a generally good time.

You see, we really don't think about water as being essential to our lives—water is essential to our fun! Pools, lakes, the beach, water parks . . . to us water means vacation.

I realize I am looking at the lake, that water source, from only one perspective—enjoyment. What if that were my only water source? What if I had to bathe in it, wash my clothes in it, and collect my drinking water from it? I believe my perspective would change.

> "Clean water, the essence of life and a birthright for everyone, must become available to all people now."
>
> Jean-Michel Cousteau[30]

And maybe that is just what we need. We need to change our perspective on water. Benjamin Franklin once said, "When the well is dry, we know the worth of water."[31]

Peter Singer is a well-known philosopher and professor. In recent years he has been named one of the one hundred most influential people by *Time* magazine. He wrote a book called *The Life You Can Save*, where he argues that for the first time in history it is now within our reach to eradicate poverty. He says that this is the right time to ask yourself, "What should I be doing to help?"

To share his thoughts on the water crisis, he presented the following story which occurred near Manchester, England, in 2007:

Jordon Lyon, a 10-year-old boy, leaped into a pond after his stepsister Bethany slipped in. He struggled to support her but went under himself. Anglers managed to pull Bethany out, but by then Jordon could no longer be seen. They raised the alarm, and two police community support officers soon arrived; they refused to enter the pond to find Jordon. He was later pulled out, but attempts at resuscitation failed. At the inquest on Jordon's death, the officers' inaction was defended on the grounds that they had not been trained to deal with such situations. The mother responded: "If you're walking down the street and you see a child drowning you automatically go in that water. . . . You don't have to be trained to jump in after a drowning child."[32]

This story that Singer presents may seem extreme. But before you dismiss it, think about the meaning for one more minute. We would never imagine standing by as an innocent child drowns. But 6,000 children died today from water-related illnesses—the equivalent of twenty jumbo jets crashing in one day.[33] And we did very little to stop it.

Out of all the research I have done on the need for clean water, and all the stories I have read and seen firsthand, a simple moment with my children really impacted me the most.

I was tucking them into bed one night, and we were reading a family devotional book. That night the reading came from Genesis 21. I am sure I had read this chapter before at some point over the years, but this time I was deep into some research on water, and I looked at this passage in a whole new light.

In Genesis 21 we read the story of Abraham and Sarah. You will remember that Sarah could not have children and had given her servant Hagar to Abraham as a wife. Hagar had a son named Ishmael, and soon after, Sarah also had a son—Isaac.

As you will also remember, things did not go well between Sarah and Hagar, and Sarah wanted Abraham to send Hagar away. Abraham was torn, but God told him to obey Sarah's wishes and promised to make a great nation out of Ishmael's descendants too.

Thankfully, the devotional did not go into all of these details, and I did not have to explain this complicated situation to my young boys. But it picked up the story where Abraham has to send Hagar and Ishmael away. He sends them off with one container of food and one of water.

They leave but quickly end up lost in the wilderness. They soon run out of water, and Ishmael gets sick. It is interesting that the Bible says that they run out of water but not food. You see, food is not always the issue, even today. Without clean water, food cannot be absorbed and digested properly, and children can still get sick and die. And that is just what happens with Ishmael.

He gets so bad that Hagar knows he is about to die unless she gets water soon. Helpless, she sits him under a tree, walks about a hundred yards away, and breaks down and cries out to God, "I don't want to see my son die!"

And then—this is the part I love—God sends an angel to Hagar and opens her eyes. When she looks up, she sees a well full of clean water. You know, God could have just taken her empty water container and filled it back up. But he gave her more than a short-term solution. He provided a long-term solution to an immediate need.

Hagar then gives Ishmael the water, and he makes a complete recovery.

As I finished this story with my kids, it hit me that thousands of years later, this story is being replayed over and over again in villages around the world. Every day mothers are forced to sit their children down and walk away because they don't want to watch them die.

But maybe we are the angels that God now wants to send and use to help meet their desperate needs.

I believe that we are.

It is hard to get our minds around the need for clean water. We may hear that over 1 billion people lack access to clean water, but numbers like that are impossible to really grasp, and it is so easy to get overwhelmed. We must focus in on the one child we can help, on the one village where we can make the difference, and on the one story that we can change, like this one told to one of our World Help partners:

My name is Carlos and I am seventy-four years old. The water in my village has always been limited because of the dry weather. When I was a boy, my parents sent me to fetch water along thorny hills, and when I did find it I was only able to carry two jugs because of my physical weakness. These two jugs only lasted us a couple of days, and often we would use it strictly for cooking, not for hygienic uses.

The years have passed and now I am a grandfather, yet I see the same scene. Each day I watch my grandchildren go in search of clean water, but now it is even more difficult because the majority of water sources have been contaminated. It is heartbreaking to see my grandchildren suffer through illnesses contracted through drinking dirty water. I hope to have the privilege to see a well and an abundance of clean water in our village one day.

People like Carlos have been waiting their entire lives for clean water. It is within our reach to help him and others. And when we do, there can be some amazing results.

Star School cares for 350 orphaned children who have been directly affected by the debilitating genocide that swept the entire nation of Rwanda in 1994. Until recently, the premises were without a water source, and the school had no option but to purchase water, which had become quite a financial burden.

We were able to drill a deep bore well at Star School through the help of a church in Thomasville, Georgia. This well provides clean, fresh drinking water to the students, as well as the surrounding community. With the funds that were formerly allocated to buy water, Star School is now able to provide its students with additional educational materials.

Working extensively to drill wells in the remote mountainous regions of Guatemala has yielded some amazing results. Without the wells, the villagers there are plagued with irritating skin conditions and hair loss from the dirty water they use from contaminated rivers. Children continually struggle with stomach illnesses and waterborne diseases that keep them from school and play. One of the most common reports we receive from villages who have now been supplied with clean water wells is the remarkable recovery from these maladies people are experiencing. Clean water improves hygiene and sanitation drastically, preventing the spread of disease and restoring health among thousands.

The village of Ambaji is situated atop a mountain deep in western India. Most of the people there are Hindu and have adopted the occupation of animal husbandry to provide for their families. They are called Bharwad, and they raise cows, buffaloes, and sheep. Availability of water is instrumental to their livelihood. Before they had a well, hours of time and much energy were spent hauling water from the bottom of the mountain on bicycles, a 2.5 mile round trip that most of them made multiple times a day. The community of 1,500 is now able to invest in their crops and livestock, giving the next generation a chance to grow and thrive. The dignity that accompanies work is one of the best gifts we could ever give.

> "There's nothing more fundamental to the human condition and global health than access to clean water and sanitation."
>
> Rep. Earl Blumenauer[34]

A well was recently dedicated in a village in Rwanda. Solar panels stand twenty feet high and pump the deep bore well so that it runs clean water uphill throughout the village. The plentiful sunshine of Africa keeps this well running. At the dedication, a woman from the village led in prayer. She said, "Lord, thank you for your wisdom that you gave to men, for we didn't know we had water under our feet."

Water is just an ordinary part of our everyday life, and yet it holds the key to life or death for millions around the world. The impact that clean and dirty water can have on children is unbelievable.

I recently received another message from my friend Brittany in Haiti. She has experienced firsthand the need for clean water in their community and has told me stories of babies and young children who suffer and die from dehydration, malnutrition, and pneumonia, all because they lack access to clean water. This is the letter she recently wrote to me about a girl named Junika:

> I've been meaning to tell you that the [cause*life*] conference and book really changed me and the way I help people. Sometimes water can seem so simple, so I overlook it as a cause for sickness, but the book really challenged me.
>
> Just days before the conference I was praying God would give me an answer on how to help this baby who is *always* sick with diarrhea, pneumonia, and malnutrition. I can't tell you how many times I've rushed her to hospitals thinking she might die that day. Well, two Sundays ago I was really scared for her life. I rushed her and her mother across the border and put her in the clinic for a few days. She had yet another horrible case of pneumonia and nonstop diarrhea that has made her completely listless and unable to stand or walk at seventeen months. During those three days I decided we didn't need to do this anymore, I just needed to change their living conditions and we could stop these emergency hospital visits. . . . I realized the dirty water she was drinking was making her body unable to fight off sickness. Water was the root. . . .
>
> I've moved her to a home near me and am buying her clean water until the well is up and running. I have taught the mother . . . about dirty water and its nasty effects. So now this little girl's life is changed and even saved. Thank you for educating even those of us who are supposed to know what we are doing.
>
> Seventeen-month-old Junika . . . One life saved because of your cause.[35]

While it has been said that "thousands have lived without love, not one without water,"[36] I believe people can experience both—not only the life-changing transformation of water but the Living Water that will never run out, never get dirty, and never be taken away.

It seems crystal clear—water really does equal life.

8

Saving a Dead Man

This is an emergency—normal rules don't apply. There are no easy good guys or bad guys. Do you think an African mother cares if drugs keeping her child alive are thanks to an iPod or a church plate? Or a Democrat or Republican? . . . So why should we? It can lead to uncomfortable bedfellows, but sometimes less sleep means you are more awake.

Bono[1]

I got in the car and we drove away. I had no idea where they were taking us, and I admit I got a little nervous. We ended up in a back alley somewhere behind the hotel. The car stopped, and the Russian young men hopped out of the car and popped open the trunk. I didn't know if we would find a body in the trunk or if I would be the next body in the trunk!

For a moment I thought I was in a spy movie. But I wasn't. It was just Russia in the 1980s.

I traveled to Russia for the first time when I was still in high school. My dad was already in Moscow leading a trip with some university students, and my sister and I were going to join him during our spring break. At seventeen years old, I was responsible for getting us both from Virginia all the way to Russia, all by myself.

We drove to Washington, DC, and boarded the plane for Moscow. We almost missed our connection in London, but we finally made it. When we left home, Virginia was experiencing an unusual heat wave that spring. It was in the 90s. But when we landed in Moscow, there was snow on the ground.

If you travel to Russia today, you will not find the Russia I experienced in the late 1980s. It was different—very different. The one thing I remember that stood out the most was the customer service, or lack of it. It simply did not exist in the country at that time. Under communism, people had no incentive to work harder and to move up in their jobs. Everyone was treated equally, and the service showed how well that belief system was working.

At that time, Russian youth were beginning to wake up to the world around them. They desperately wanted all things American, and jeans and backpacks were at the top of their list. You could trade these items for Russian trinkets and souvenirs.

I was excited about being able to trade, so I made sure I brought lots of jeans and backpacks. I headed down to the lobby of the hotel with one of the university students to meet two Russian young men who were waiting for us and ready to make the trade. However, when we got to the lobby they asked us to come outside. They did not want to do it in the hotel lobby. We followed them outside. Then they asked us to get in their car. So we did. I know, right now you are saying to yourself, "What was she thinking?" I am saying that to myself too! All I can say is, there are a lot of things you do at seventeen that you would never do now.

When our car ended up in that back alley and the trunk popped open, I was surprised and relieved to see it filled with Russian novelties—it could have been something much worse! That day I traded my simple jeans and backpacks for an authentic Russian military coat and hat, complete with all the medals and awards given to the young man who once wore it. I still have it today.

> "To me, a faith in Jesus Christ that is not aligned with the poor . . . it's nothing."
>
> Bono[2]

My adventures in Russia were just that—adventures. But things were starting to change, and they would change faster than any of us thought possible. The Iron Curtain was coming down, and freedom was about to spring forth.

In high school I gave a speech on Gorbachev, perestroika, and glasnost. These movements of openness and restructuring are said to have led to the dissolution of the Soviet Union. I never realized that just a few years later, on another trip, I would be experiencing firsthand the complexity of these words in an ever-changing Russian government.

We were confined to our hotel and told not to leave. My then fiancé and parents were watching CNN at home and seeing footage of military tanks in the streets of Moscow and bombs being fired at the Russian White House. Thousands of protestors had gathered in the streets. Russia was on the brink of civil war, and my family thought I was right in the middle of it.

Actually, I was right down the road at the Cosmos hotel. And while I was confined to the hotel, I was perfectly fine. But looking back on this today, I realize that I was right in the middle of it. I was in Russia during one of the most turbulent times of its history.

It was still a volatile time in Russia when I first visited Cancer Hospital #62 just outside of Moscow. It was the leading cancer hospital in all of Russia at the time. But even the top doctors could not make up for the lack of resources, medicine, and supplies. People were sent here to die.

The first time I visited Cancer Hospital #62, I was with my dad. It was a hard visit. He had survived cancer only a few years earlier, and the visit brought back painful memories. After sixteen surgeries, and with the doctors giving him only a 20 percent chance to survive, a cancer hospital was the last place he wanted to be.

We noticed that the hospital was getting by on almost nothing. The medicine cabinets were empty, there were no bandages for wounds, and straws were being used for tracheotomies. In fact, each night two people washed rubber latex gloves so that they could be reused the next day. Yes, that's what I said—reused!

The chief surgeon was a man named Dr. Mahkson. He asked us to help, and my dad promised him that we would. Using the help of government grants, we were able to ship thirteen ocean-going containers full of supplies valued at over two million dollars!

I was able to be there the week that one of these containers was delivered. I literally saw doctors running out of surgery, ripping open the boxes, and pulling out tubing or some piece of equipment that they needed for surgery right at that moment. It was incredible.

Dr. Mahkson came up to me and said, "Young lady, please give your dad a message. Tell him thank you, and tell him that you are the first Americans to ever keep their promise!"

On one of our last visits to Cancer Hospital #62, Dr. Mahkson told my dad, "At first I did not believe your faith. But I have seen it in action. I now accept your faith."

Pretend for a minute that you are sitting at a café enjoying a nice cup of coffee and your favorite pastry. You look around and notice a thrift store and hardware store nearby and a large warehouse across the street. The friend you are sitting with tells you that the warehouse is home to about twenty-five homeless people. As you are sitting there, you see smoke start to rise from the warehouse. Everyone quickly realizes that the warehouse is on fire. The doors are locked and the windows are barred. What do you do?

Option 1: Do nothing—they're homeless. Carry on your business, enjoy your pastries, and do not concern yourself with others.

Option 2: Pray. Just pray.

Option 3: Offer food from the café. They are going to be hungry when they get out of that building.

Option 4: Offer clothing from the thrift store. This will help meet their physical needs and provide for what they lose in the fire.

Option 5: Offer tracts and Bibles from the Christian bookstore. You can shove them between the bars on the windows. Some may burn in the fire, but some of the people may be able to read them. After all, if they are going to die, at least they can die knowing God.

Option 6: Rush into the hardware store and get the necessary tools to break the locks or bars on the windows, then race over and rescue those who are trapped in the warehouse.

A friend shared a version of this story above with me. I have taken great liberty with it and added a few options of my own. But I have not been able to get it out of my mind. It is a great example of the debate that has sprung up in the faith community on the issue of helping the poor and disenfranchised. Recent books have fueled the fire and caused people of faith to reevaluate their mission and methods when it comes to helping. This is not a bad thing. But too much theory and not enough action is never a good thing either.

As obvious as the answer seems to me, if you sat a few people down and asked them what option they would choose, you might get a few different answers. None of us would admit to option 1, although that is exactly what we do many times—nothing.

Option 2 may seem just as absurd—to do nothing but pray. But we often do. Prayer is extremely important and needed. But prayer alone is never what God intended. My dad always taught me to pray as if it all depended on God but to work as if it all depended on me.

Now, options 3 through 6 are where things get a little tricky. All of these options are needed, but they may all be needed at different times. And timing is everything.

The people who survive will need food and clothing.

And the people who survive will be searching for hope. What better time to introduce them to God's love?

But that is the key phrase: the people who survive. If I were choosing between these options, I would choose option 6. I would use whatever tools I could find in that hardware store to break in to that building and set as many people free as possible. My goal would be to save their lives.

All around the world, people are trapped in the burning buildings of poverty, hunger, disease, abuse, slavery, and spiritual darkness. Their worlds are burning down around them. We have many options for how to help. But I choose to start by saving their lives, because in the end, you can't save a dead man.

> "If you haven't noticed, people are dying. It's an emergency."
> Jeffrey Sachs[3]

In her book *Global Soccer Mom*, Shayne Moore says,

> In the political world, the term "social justice" is often used to describe the activities of working to eradicate injustices such as poverty and disease. In our churches we use the word

missions or missional. Historically, mission departments in churches were about spreading the gospel message and conversion, with a smaller focus on meeting the physical real-life needs of people around the world. In fact, in the conservative faith tradition I grew up in, "social justice" and "activism" are scary terms used to describe liberals. However, when I consider that 16,000 children die every day from malnutrition and extreme poverty, or that more than 1 billion people live on less than $2 a day, social justice no longer sounds like a secular or church issue, conservative or liberal issue. When I consider that gender-based violence against women and girls is pervasive in the developing world and that women and girls are marginalized and exploited in situations of extreme poverty, advocating or speaking up on their behalf no longer looks like a Democrat or Republican issue. It seems to me to be a compassion issue.[4]

When I was growing up, traditional "missions" focused primarily on evangelism. Today, people of faith are beginning to see the incredible need for a more holistic approach. Without access to clean water, food, and medicine that the body needs, faith means very little. But without the faith that feeds the soul, the short-term needs of today are nothing but a quick fix. When we focus on both—body and soul—something incredible happens. Hope is restored.

Christian Buckley and Ryan Dobson say in their book *Humanitarian Jesus*,

In 1854, Charles Spurgeon began preaching in London. The city was engulfed with such poverty and social injustice that just a decade later, another London minister, William Booth, left his pulpit and walked out into the streets, founding what would become the Salvation Army to reach the poor, homeless, hungry and destitute. It was in this London on June 18, 1876, Spurgeon preached the following words:

"Men have enough practical sense always to judge that if professed Christians do not care for their bodily wants, there cannot be much sincerity in their zeal for men's souls. If a man will give me spiritual food in the form of a tract, but would not give me a piece of bread for my body, how can I think much of him?" . . .

Perhaps from these words, Spurgeon was believed to have said, "If you want to give a hungry man a tract, then wrap it up in a sandwich." . . .

Every encounter between God and us has these two dimensions—the physical and the spiritual.[5]

I believe in this so strongly that World Help's mission statement is based on this very principle. World Help exists to provide help for today and hope for tomorrow in impoverished communities around the world. We focus on both the physical and the spiritual because we believe they cannot and should not be separated.

"How was Haiti?" I must have been asked that question a thousand times. And I'm still not sure how to answer.

The images on television did not do the devastation justice. You really did have to see it for yourself to fully understand how debilitated this country was. Driving down the streets, I saw house after house and building after building completely destroyed. But unlike on a TV screen, in real life the devastation has no end. It simply goes on and on.

We were told that at the time 75 percent of the people in Port-au-Prince were living in tents, and I could tell that was true when I flew in. From the window of the plane all I could see was blue on the ground—blue tarps and tents acting as makeshift shelters. And with the sweltering heat during the day and the rainy season, living in those tents was even more difficult.

In Port-au-Prince we passed by the Presidential Palace, and I snapped a photo. I could not get over the fact that months after the quake, nothing had been done to repair it. This is the equivalent of our White House, and it had sat there destroyed for months.

The bodies had been removed from the streets of Port-au-Prince, for the most part, but the rubble remained. It was estimated that it would take four million truckloads to clean out all the debris . . . four million!

I came home and tried to describe to my husband what it was like. I told him to imagine an earthquake like this happening in New York City and all the buildings collapsing. Then imagine if all of the survivors set up tents on the streets in between the demolished buildings. If you can picture that—the crowds, the chaos, the filth, the unsanitary conditions—then you have pictured Haiti after the quake.

Governments were arguing over the best way to help Haiti. Large aid organizations were pulling out, and we heard that the Red Cross would soon stop delivering water to the tent cities. And Americans were losing interest.

In any disaster, the children are always the ones who suffer the most. At least 1.5 million children were affected by the earthquake in Haiti. But children in Haiti have been suffering for years. One in seven children dies before their fifth birthday. Even before the earthquake, 60 percent of children lacked access to even basic health care—children like little Marie Joy.

This beautiful little two-year-old girl was thrown into a fire when the earthquake struck. Her left arm was consumed. She was actually found in the rubble and thought to be dead. For three weeks, she sat without help and without medical attention. When she was finally rescued, her arm was like charcoal.

When I met Marie Joy, she was an extremely shy and withdrawn little girl. Not only was her arm healing, but emotionally she was beginning to heal too. She has now made a full recovery and turned into a bubbly and happy child, but the harsh reality is, she would not have survived had she not been rescued.

A little baby boy was born two days after the earthquake. His father was killed in the disaster. His distraught mother was overwhelmed and did not know what to do. Out of desperation, she thought the best thing to do was to give up her baby. She brought him to Danita's Children in northern Haiti. But they convinced this desperate mother to stay with her baby. They took them both in and named this precious little boy Josiah, which means, "God will save."

I had the privilege of holding little Josiah as they told me his incredible story. Tears filled my eyes as I realized I was holding a little miracle baby—a survivor.

"There are people in the world so hungry that God cannot appear to them except in the form of bread."

Mohandas Ghandi[6]

And then there was Lonique. This little seven-year-old boy lost his home, his father, and his entire left arm when the earthquake struck. He spent three weeks in a makeshift hospital tent. When he was found, he had a piece of duct tape on his forehead with instructions for the next doctor. He had no medical charts—just a piece of tape. Every time the wind would blow into the tent, Lonique would scream, worried that another earthquake was about to hit.

Lonique is now making a full recovery. He has a long road ahead of him, but he also has hope.

In a country where half the population is children, there are hundreds of thousands of orphans. Before the earthquake, there were almost half a million. No one knows what the number has grown to now.

Immediately following the quake, World Help identified several hundred children, already living in children's homes, who desperately needed help. They now go to school outside under tents and sleep outside too, because their buildings are damaged. While they still need new buildings, we have been able to help meet their most basic needs during these crucial months. By providing food, water, clothing, and supplies, we have given them a chance to survive.

These are actually the lucky children. Many others are still waiting.

At the tent city supported by Sean Penn in Port-au-Prince, thousands of tents covered what used to be a golf course. I met a group of three eleven-year-old boys there. All three had lost family in the earthquake. One could not speak at all. Another, a boy named Stevenson, had already been abandoned by his father and had now lost his mother in the quake. Wearing scant clothing and torn shoes, these boys were doing whatever they could to occupy their time and keep their mind off reality. They needed hope more than anything—hope for a better future.

In the days and months following the earthquake in Haiti, the priority was survival. That was not the end, just the starting point. Meeting physical needs must come first sometimes. In that way, not only do we "earn the right to be heard," but we show that God really cares about our whole life. As Gabe Lyons says, "In the lives of the mistreated, underrepresented, and left behind of our world, the Christian responds by solving real problems. Their acts of social justice demonstrate to the world that Christ cares about the here and now—not just the afterlife."[7]

I have seen physical suffering around the world, but I have also seen spiritual suffering. I've seen the incredible need for Bibles and even people copying pages from the Bible by hand, just so they could have a copy of God's Word. People are physically and spiritually suffering, but our approach to helping does not have to be either-or.

Years ago I read a book by Jim Collins called *Built to Last*. In it he explains the "Genius of the AND." In talking about highly visionary companies, he says that they

do not oppress themselves with what we call the "Tyranny of the OR"—the rational view that cannot easily accept paradox, that cannot live with two seemingly contradictory forces or ideas at the same time. The "Tyranny of the OR" pushes people to believe that things must be either A OR B, but *not both*. It makes such proclamations as:

- "You can have change *OR* stability."
- "You can be conservative *OR* liberal."
- "You can have low cost *OR* high quality." . . .

Instead of being oppressed by the "Tyranny of the OR," highly visionary companies liberate themselves with the "Genius of the AND"—the ability to embrace both extremes of a number of dimensions at the same time. Instead of choosing between A *OR* B, they figure out a way to have both A *AND* B.[8]

In this great debate between helping physically and helping spiritually, I think a "both/and" approach would serve us all well. While over 1 billion people live in extreme poverty, we write books on whether it is more important to feed a hungry child or to share the gospel. While 29,000 children around the world die every day from preventable diseases, we debate the issue of dependency. Wouldn't it be refreshing and effective if we put our energy toward doing both? What if we focused on saving the body *and* the soul?

People of faith should clearly see by Jesus's example to us that he was truly concerned with the physical needs of those he came in contact with. He was not only concerned about their souls. Instead, he fed them, touched them, and healed them. He met real needs—both physical and spiritual.

Jerry Wiles, president of Living Water, said,

To paraphrase an African head of state, "You can't minister to dead people. You can't do health care to dead people. You can't educate dead people. You've got to have them alive first." The first thing is to bring physical life. It is true that if you just bring the water without the message, you just extend their physical life. It's not a matter of either-or with us. It's both-and in every case. It's not a choice.[9]

There are many things we disagree about in our churches, and that will probably not change anytime soon. So much precious time is wasted on issues that in the end really don't matter. But there is one point that we should agree on, one thing that should unite us all. We should all be able to agree on the importance of reaching out to the poor and needy—to share our food with the hungry, to give shelter to the homeless, and to give clothes to those who need them (see Isa. 58:7). Because when we do, God's love is poured out on a hurting world.

I echo the words of Max Lucado when I say, "May the poor bless you because of me, and may my efforts somehow reduce the number of poor."[10]

9

Boring, Safe,
or Significant

*Are you bored with life? Then throw your-
self into some work you believe in with all
your heart, live for it, die for it, and you will
find happiness that you had thought could
never be yours.*

Dale Carnegie

I seemed to watch him every night. He simply had the best coverage of the earthquake in Haiti. But the reason I watched him was not just because he did a good job cover-ing the story—I knew he cared about the story.

Yes, I am a fan of Anderson Cooper. I am not condoning his beliefs or his lifestyle, and I really don't know that much about him. But ever since I read his book *Dispatches from the Edge*, I have been a fan.

Few people know that he is the son of Gloria Vanderbilt, and even fewer know the hard and painful life he has led. In his book he talks about his father dying while undergoing heart bypass surgery at only fifty years old. Anderson was only ten. Years later he would have to face the tragic suicide of his close brother. This painful life combined with his interest in the world has led to his informative and compassionate coverage of the most devastating disasters of our time.

One night I was watching his coverage of Haiti after the earthquake. He was in the streets during the time when people were literally going crazy. Prisoners had escaped from jail, looters were running rampant, and the sheer chaos and fear of the unknown was making people behave in ways they never would have before. During his coverage you could see destruction all around him. Of course getting the story was most important at the time, and he had a job to do. But then something special happened.

The streets were being blocked off, and a little boy was being separated from his family on the other side of the barricade. The little boy was crying and obviously hurt—he was bleeding. Anderson stopped his coverage and, giving no thought to his own safety, bent down, picked up the boy, and handed him over the barricade to the relative safety of his family.

Okay, he had me. He was much more than a reporter now, much more than a journalist. He showed that he actually cared about what he was reporting on. I remember an African principal telling my dad once, "We don't care how much you know until we know how much you care." What a powerful statement, and one that Anderson was proving. I now knew how much he cared, and it made an impact on me.

In our lives people are watching to see how much we really care. So often we let them down and fall flat on our face. Our busy lifestyles and fear hold us back and keep us from reaching out. Consider this story:

I heard of an experiment a small band of seminary students carried out on fellow members of their class some time ago. I know it is true because I later spoke with one of the men involved. The class was given an assignment on Luke 10:30–37, the familiar account of the Good Samaritan. The assignment was due the next day. Most of the men in that class traveled along the same pathway leading to the classroom the next morning. One of the seminarians in the experiment wore old, torn clothing, disguised himself as though he had been beaten and bruised, and placed himself along the path, clearly in view of all the young students making their way back to class. With their assignments neatly written, carefully documented, and tucked under their arms, not one seminarian so much as paused to come to his assistance to wipe the catsup off his neck and chest.

Intellectually, the assignment on love and caring was completed. But personally? Well, you decide![1]

This story, as captured in Chuck Swindoll's book *Come Before Winter and Share My Hope*, was actually a famous research project performed by Princeton students back in the 1970s. It was re-created recently by ABC News for their "What Would You Do?" series. Their goal was to answer this question: "For every hero who saved a stranger, how many other people saw the same situation and did nothing?"

They put out a casting call for an "on-camera tryout" for ABC News. When the applicants arrived, they were told that they would have to discuss a topic on camera. While the applicants thought they were all getting random topics, in fact they were each given the same—the Good Samaritan story from the Bible. I am sure you are familiar with this story of the man who was beaten by thieves and left to die on the side of the road. After two religious men came by and did nothing, a third man, a Samaritan, stopped to care for him and even paid for his care until he was well (see Luke 10:30–37).

After the applicants received their topics, they were given directions to a studio where they would have their audition. Unbeknownst to them, on the way to the studio they would pass a person (an actor) in great distress and clearly in need of help.

The producers wondered what the results would be but thought, "Who better to come to their aid than someone with the biblical story of helping one's fellow man echoing in their ears?"

Unfortunately, many of the twenty-two participants did not stop. They walked right past the actor, arrived at the studio, and gave their passionate speech on the Good Samaritan. Why? Well, it was a chance to be on television, and they were in a hurry. Time pressure was found to be a significant deterrent to stopping.

But there was another reason—fear. Maybe it was the race of the actor or the way he was acting that made some of them feel uncomfortable. One of the applicants said he felt threatened, and "if you are scared of the person, the fear alone will deter you."

> "The first question which the priest and the Levite asked was: 'If I stop to help this man, what will happen to me?' But . . . the good Samaritan reversed the question: 'If I do not stop to help this man, what will happen to him?'"
>
> Martin Luther King Jr.[2]

However, the experiment cited one woman whose concern far outweighed her fear. She ran all the way back to her car to get her cell phone to help the man, even though she suffered from asthma. Her actions were hailed as the "most perfect demonstration of the Good Samaritan story."[3]

I don't know about you, but those "What Would You Do?" shows always scare me, because I wonder what I would do. I think I know what I would do, and I like to believe that I would act and behave a certain way in these situations. But the truth is, I don't really know. Factors like time and fear really do affect the way we live and the decisions we make.

Fear can be a useful instinct that helps to protect us. But more often than not, it becomes a harmful addiction that holds us back and keeps us from living out our best life and our most unique story. In his book *A Million Miles in a Thousand Years*, Donald Miller says, "Fear isn't only a guide to keep us safe; it's also a manipulative emotion that can trick us into living a boring life."[4]

Do you want to be safe, or do you really want to change the world? The conflict is that we want to be brave, we want to take risks . . . but we also want to be safe. The problem is, we can't have it both ways.

We want the American dream: to graduate from high school, go to college, get a degree, and then what? Find the love of your life and get married. Then what? Get a job. Then what? Buy a car, buy a house, buy life insurance. Then what? Grow old and retire. Then what? Is that it? Is that all there is?

In fact, couldn't we just sum up the entire American dream in the single word "safety"? That's what it's all about. No matter what you want out of life, you can achieve it in America in comfort, style, and in the end, safety. But there is a problem. We cannot be safe and take risks at the same time.

Eleanor Roosevelt said, "You gain strength, courage and confidence by every experience in which you really stop to look fear in the face. You must do the thing which you think you cannot do"[5] and "Do something every day that scares you."[6]

This can get messy. It gets uncomfortable. It means touching people who are dying of diseases. It means going to the filthy slums, the garbage dumps, the places we would never normally go . . . just to reach that one hurting person.

You could argue that we all take risks every day. We take a risk every time we get in a car. We take a risk every time we fly. There is really an element of risk in everything we do. Some people experience more risk than others. But no matter what you do or where you live, the reality is, there is an element of risk in everything that we do.

So we must answer this question: Do we want to stay safe, or do we want to change the world? We can't have it both ways.

I wish I could say that I am fearless, that I am one of those people who does not worry about anything. But I'm not. I do get scared and I do worry.

My good friend Danita Estrella, who founded Danita's Children in northern Haiti as a single young American woman, told me this: "People think that I can do what I do because I am not afraid. But they are wrong. I just do it afraid."

That has become a motto to me of sorts. When I am feeling scared to do what I believe God has called me to do, I don't let the fear hold me back. I just do it scared.

I don't remember having so much fear when I was young, but marriage and family does something to change your level of risk tolerance. However, too often we simply use our family as an excuse.

A few years ago I helped write a book on children who have been affected by HIV/AIDS. At the time, statistics showed that Christians were the least likely group to help AIDS victims in Africa, and less than 3 percent of evangelicals said that they would help a Christian organization minister to an AIDS orphan.[7] I wondered how this could be possible.

Was it because many people still believed that AIDS is only a disease of homosexuals, prostitutes, and drug users? Was it because many in the church had chosen to believe that AIDS is God's judgment for sin? Was it that we simply did not yet understand that most of the people affected by AIDS are innocent women and children? Or was it just because the whole idea and topic of AIDS made us completely uncomfortable and, well, scared?

David Platt writes in his book *Radical*,

> For the sake of more than a billion people today who have yet to hear the gospel, I want to risk it all. For the sake of the twenty-six thousand children who will die today of starvation or preventable disease, I want to risk it all. For the sake of an increasingly marginalized and relatively ineffective church in our culture, I want to risk it all. For the sake of my life, my family, and the people who surround me, I want to risk it all.[8]

The great missionary J. Hudson Taylor said, "Unless there is an element of risk in your exploits for God, there is no need for faith."[9]

You see, I believe we have a choice. We can choose to be safe and lead a really boring life. Or we can choose to live a life of significance—a life that takes risks for the sake of changing the world.

We all have heroes. As children they are superheroes, sports figures, and movie stars. They change as we grow older . . . sometimes. But my son has a hero that I hope he keeps for a long time.

My nine-year-old son Bentley is a true Chicago Cubs fan! All you need to do is take one step in his room (or what we like to call the Cubs shrine) to see his dedication to his favorite baseball team. But what was just a childhood obsession turned into true fanaticism when he visited Wrigley Field in Chicago this past August. Not only did he visit, but he got to actually meet many of the players, including his favorite, Carlos Zambrano, a former pitcher for the Cubs. He also was able to go to batting practice and

> "Life is either a daring adventure or nothing at all."
> Helen Keller[10]

even warm up with the team on the field. This would have been a dream come true for a grown man, but for a nine-year-old boy—he might as well have won a million dollars. He was ecstatic!

It took weeks for him to come down from his baseball high, and even now when you mention that day, his eyes still light up. I am so happy that he got to experience that, and I am so happy that he has a childhood hero in Zambrano.

Carlos Zambrano is not your average baseball player. Yes, professionally he has had his share of struggles, but in his downtime, he travels to Guatemala to help rescue dying babies and children from the remote hills and bring them to the baby rescue center that we support at Hope of Life. His financial support is helping to complete a state-of-the-art children's hospital that will literally save thousands of children's lives in Guatemala for years to come.

Well, as a humanitarian mom whose interest in baseball is limited . . . I think Zambrano may just become my hero too!

I have to tell you my favorite part of this ongoing story, though. At Christmas, Bentley saw our Gifts of Hope catalog. Flipping through it, he decided that he wanted to provide a goat for a needy family for Christmas. In some countries, giving a goat is the equivalent of giving a family a new car. It would cost them half a year's income to buy it themselves. A goat provides fresh milk every day and helps a family become more self-sufficient.

Bentley took all of his own money that he had been saving and gave $100 to provide a goat. I have to admit, I was so proud—he was "getting it," and at a very early age.

What made this so much more special was that Zambrano was actually in Guatemala when Bentley's goat was being delivered. Bentley's photo of Zambrano at Wrigley Field serves as a constant reminder of the impact his hero made on his life. A new photo of Zambrano and Bentley's goat will be a constant reminder of the difference Bentley was able to make in the lives of others.

Zambrano has enough money to live any kind of life he wants. He could easily choose a safe and comfortable life, far away from the needs of suffering children and families. He may not be perfect, and you may see him lose his temper from time to time in the dugout. But he has chosen to live a life of significance, a life that even the youngest of fans can look up to.

I have learned that together, a baseball hero, a little boy, and a goat really can do a world of good. But it requires a choice—a choice to lead a significant life.

As parents, we have this responsibility not only in our own lives but also in the lives of the children we are trying to raise. In his book *Just Courage*, Gary Haugen addresses the question of "Are we raising our children to be successful or significant?" He says,

After we have poured into our children all the good food and shelter and clothing, after we have provided them with great education, discipline, structure and love, after we have worked so hard to provide every good thing, they turn to us and ask, "Why have you given all this to me?"

And the honest answer from me is, "So you'll be safe." And my kids look up at me and say, "Really? That's it? You want me to be safe? Your grand ambition for me is that nothing bad happens?" . . . According to Jesus, it doesn't have to be that way. He gives me a role in helping my kids choose to be brave, to be loving and to be significant. In the end, this is the stuff that will change the world.[11]

Do you remember what it was like to wonder what you would be when you grew up? As children we were asked about this over and over. It forced us to really think about it and come up with the coolest answer possible: astronaut, policeman, professional athlete, actress on Broadway, or even president of the United States! We dreamed big and never thought for a moment that those dreams were beyond our reach.

It occurred to me recently that no one has asked me that question in a long time. No one seems to care anymore about what I want to be when I grow up. I suppose they assume that I must have already arrived at that special place—the place where you are doing exactly what you were born to do.

But do we ever really arrive at that special place? Or is life more of a journey of twists and turns that keep teaching us and preparing us for all God has in store?

When my son Riley was nine he informed me of his future plans. He told me that he wanted to be a missionary—a missionary that helps animals. I thought this was so sweet and so representative of his personality and heart. He has a heart and passion for the world and people in need. He also has a heart for animals. He used to love Animal Planet, and his favorite show was *Meerkat Manor*. He stopped watching, though, because he just couldn't take the harsh reality of nature the show depicted. Every time one of the meerkats died, he simply fell apart.

> "Our greatest fear should not be that we fail, but that we succeed in something that does not matter."
>
> Daniel Henderson[12]

I have to admit, when I heard him say, "a missionary who helps animals," my first thought was, "Well, that's an interesting combination." But then I thought, "Why not?"

I know that in a few years, what he wants to be when he grows up will most likely change and that this is just one step along his journey. But it was nice to remember that feeling and excitement of dreaming big—even if it doesn't quite make sense yet.

Donald Miller says,

If I have a hope, it's that God sat over the dark nothing and wrote you and me, specifically, into the story, and put us in with the sunset and the rainstorm as though to say, *Enjoy your place in my story. The beauty of it means you matter, and you can create within it even as I have created you.*

I've wondered, though, if one of the reasons we fail to acknowledge the brilliance of life is because we don't want the responsibility inherent in the acknowledgment. We don't want to be characters in a story because characters have to move and breathe and face conflict with courage. And if life isn't remarkable, then we don't have to do any of that; we can be unwilling victims rather than grateful participants.[13]

When I think about facing fear, I think of a pastor from Iraq. He has shared some incredible stories from his life in Baghdad. Life there for him was anything but simple, and things to be thankful for were few and far between.

When his family needed to go to the store to buy groceries and supplies, he and his wife had to make a choice—who would go? It was not because it was a dreaded task but because they knew that they lived in a dangerous city where bombs frequently go off unexpectedly. They wanted to make sure that if anything happened, at least one of them would still be alive to take care of their children. Can you imagine? I can't believe I complain about going to the store.

One day he was getting ready to take his son to school. He noticed that his son's backpack looked a little bigger than normal. He opened it to find a pair of pajamas and a few personal items resting on top of the schoolbooks. He asked his son why he was taking these things to school. His son explained that if something happened to his parents while he was at school, maybe it would be easier to find someone to take care of him if he already had his own pajamas. I can't imagine my children going to school with these kinds of fears going through their heads.

Not all of us are called to face these kinds of fears and risks. But we are all called to live our best life: a life that uses all the gifts and abilities God has given us, a life that is lived out of the shadow of fear.

Your life is a story—a great story. But you can choose how that story is told. To live a great story, you will surely have to face some kind of risk, hardship, and even pain. But if you are able to look back on a significant life—a life lived fully awake, a life that has changed lives—I believe it will all be worth it. Don't you?

10

Let's Roll

There may be times when we are powerless to prevent injustice, but there must never be a time when we fail to protest.

Elie Wiesel[1]

Osama Bin Laden is dead and justice has been done."[2] Hillary Clinton spoke those words on the morning of May 2, 2011, nearly ten years after the horrific events of 9/11. As I was driving and listening to her speak on the radio, I began to think about that tragic day in September and the images, scenes, and words that we will never forget. The man who had invoked so much death and destruction on our country was finally brought to justice and given what he deserved.

On that tragic day in September 2001, a young father from New Jersey stood up to the terror on United Flight 93. He was not alone in his fight, but his last recorded words made him a hero even in death.

The actual recording indicates that he said, "Are you ready? Okay, let's roll."[3] With all respect, I just can't help but think that Todd Beamer must have been such a cool guy. I mean, what kind of person in the midst of such chaos and terror would say something like "Let's roll"? I think it further proves the kind of person he must have been.

"That is 'so Todd,'" his widow writes. "It showed he felt he could still do something positive in the midst of a crisis."

It was his phrase to get his sons going. She said, "When they heard, 'Let's roll,' they'd head for the door."[4]

His words became a rallying call for Americans in the war on terror. In fact, US Air Force planes across the nation had the phrase "Let's Roll" inscribed on them.[5] And for many of us who watched the events of 9/11 unfold, "Let's roll" will forever remind us to stand up for what we believe, for what is good, and for all that we hold dear. Todd was determined to fight for what he believed, no matter the consequences. And although he lost his life, because he fought, countless others were saved.

In order for justice to "roll," we have to be willing to fight—no matter the cost.

This word *justice* has been intriguing me for some time now. It is often misunderstood, and it is a word that can bring both fear and hope. My husband is a judge at the highest trial court level in the Commonwealth of Virginia. He knows all too well the legal meaning of justice. He interprets the laws and dispenses justice on a daily basis. His decisions often bring relief and closure to some and shame and despair to others.

I think many people are confused about what justice means. Some think of it simply in legal terms as someone getting what they deserve—justice being served. Because of this, they don't see this as a fitting term for meeting the needs of the poor and disenfranchised around the world.

Timothy Keller says in his book *Generous Justice*,

Many readers may be asking at this point why we are calling private giving to the poor "justice." Some Christians believe that justice is strictly *misphat*—the punishment of wrongdoing, period. This does not mean that they think that believers should be indifferent to the plight of the poor, but they would insist that helping the needy through generous giving should be called mercy, compassion, or charity, not justice. In English, however, the word "charity" conveys a good but optional activity. Charity cannot be a requirement, for then it would not be charity. But this view does not fit in with the strength or balance of the Biblical teaching.

In the Scripture, gifts to the poor are called "acts of righteousness," as in Matthew 6:1–2. Not giving generously, then, is not stinginess, but unrighteousness, a violation of God's law. Also, we looked at Job's description of all the things he was doing in order to live a just and righteous life in Job 31. He calls every failure to help the poor a sin, offensive to God's splendor (verse 23) and deserving of judgment and punishment (verse 28). Remarkably, Job is asserting that it would be a sin against God to think of his goods as belonging to himself alone. To not "share his bread" and his assets with the poor would be unrighteous, a sin against God, and therefore by definition a violation of God's justice.[6]

Understanding the true meaning of justice carries responsibility but ultimately leads to hope.

Imagine with me, if you will, a river. Not just any river but a powerful river. This river is charging down from the top of a huge mountain. As Mike and Danae Yankoski put it, "Boulders, trees, and even the foothills of the mountain cannot block its path for long. The river is persistent and dauntless. Given enough time, water will overcome any obstacle and continue its endless journey."[7]

The book of Amos says that justice should "roll on like a river, righteousness like a never-failing stream" (5:24 NIV). So justice should continue always and never disappoint, grow tired, or weaken. Justice should roll.

But this passage tells us something else equally important:

> I can't stand your religious meetings.
> I'm fed up with your conferences and conventions.

I want nothing to do with your religion projects,
    your pretentious slogans and goals.
I'm sick of your fund-raising schemes,
    your public relations and image making.
I've had all I can take of your noisy ego-music.
    When was the last time you sang to me?
Do you know what I want?
    I want justice—oceans of it.
I want fairness—rivers of it.
    That's what I want. That's all I want. (Amos 5:23–24 Message)

We go to church every week, we attend Christian conferences and events, and we sing our songs of praise. And all the while we forget to be a mighty flood of justice to those in need.

Eugene Peterson says, "Justice is a serious gospel-prophetic mandate. Far too many Christians for too long have left the cause to others."[8] Justice is important to God and reflects his character. As Keller says, "God loves and defends those with the least economic and social power, and so should we. That is what it means to 'do justice.'"[9] In fact, it has been said that when we deny justice, we are actually "hiding God's beauty from the world."[10]

God's beauty was hidden when most of the world turned their backs on the country of Rwanda. In the midst of terror and destruction, a little girl named Josianne had her life turned upside down.

She told me, "Almost everyone I knew was gone. I had a family. My mom and dad and relatives, we had a large family. But then my dad was killed and my relatives were killed. Those who lived near us were killed."

Josianne, her mother, and her three-year-old sister were the only ones to escape the brutality. When they returned to their home, they found it all but destroyed. "Mom couldn't repair our home, so she went into the village to find a man to help. One day, while Mom was home alone, the man raped her. He also infected her with HIV and made her pregnant," Josianne said.

After Josianne's sister was born, her mother got very sick and eventually died. At fifteen years old, Josianne became mother to her two sisters. She feeds and clothes them but struggles to find a way to pay for medication for the youngest. I could sense she had grown up way too fast. At only twenty-four years old, she acts much older and has the responsibilities and burdens of a woman twice her age. I asked Josianne if she had any dreams or goals for her life. She said, "My mission is to bring up my young sisters and make sure they grow up and become individuals and establish a family."

There is no greater example of the deadly combination of violence, genocide, prejudice, poverty, and HIV/AIDS than in the small central African country of Rwanda.[11] How can we ever forget that in a country with a population of only 9 million, almost 1 million men, women, and children were massacred in 1994—in just four months?[13] The impact of this destruction still echoes throughout this broken nation. Josianne and her sisters are among more than 1 million orphans living in Rwanda as a result of both the 1994 genocide and the growing impact of HIV/AIDS.[14] It is the rule rather than the exception to see older siblings like Josianne raising younger children.

> "When the history of our times is written, will we be remembered as the generation that turned our backs in a moment of a global crisis or will it be recorded that we did the right thing?"
>
> Nelson Mandela[12]

The rest of the world found out about the tragedies of this genocide through news reports and headlines. But Josianne saw it firsthand. She was only twelve years old when the slaughter began.

Between April and July of 1994, members of the Hutu ethnic group conducted deliberate and systematic assassinations of ethnic Tutsis and moderate Hutus. From this dark time in history came some of the most horrific stories and brutal images that many of us have ever seen. The butchers wanted to eliminate the entire Tutsi ethnic group while inflicting as much pain as possible. Murderous mobs used machetes, clubs with nails, axes, knives, and poles to hack and bludgeon unarmed people. Guns, while available, were rarely used because gunshot deaths were not painful enough.[15]

One Rwandan woman told World Help how she had been captured and her family killed. She was cut so severely that she was left to die on the road. She suffered alone in severe pain for three days until she was found and taken to a hospital. "I know all the people who did this to me. They were our immediate neighbors. I spoke to them, and they gave me time to pray for them before they started cutting me. I prayed for them until I lost consciousness. I know it was the devil that led them to do such an abomination, and I pray the Lord to save their souls from perdition."

All Hutus were encouraged to take part in the massacre, or at the very least not interfere or offer help to the Tutsis. Teachers turned on their students. Doctors refused to treat the wounded. Some children were forced to murder their friends or neighbors. Hutu women who had married Tutsis were made to kill their own children. Even the church as a whole turned a blind eye to the tragedy until it was too late. Some heroic individuals bravely did what they could to save lives. But noncompliant Hutus who protested or stepped in to help were threatened and then executed—priests, nuns, officials, businessmen—no one was safe.[16]

Hutu leaders were intent on total annihilation. There were to be no survivors. Armed killers searched hospitals, homes, fields, streams, forests, and swamps for escapees. Many families fled to local churches for safety. Bloodthirsty mobs threw grenades into the buildings and shot or cut up those who were still alive.

I visited one such church in Ruhanga and heard this horrific story. The congregation had been a mix of Hutus and

Tutsis. When the killings began, women and children fled into the church, while men tried to fight the attackers outside. But church members began fighting each other! The pastor was murdered by an elder because he refused to divide his congregation between Hutus and Tutsis. As he lay dying on the front steps of the church, 4,000 people, mostly women and children, were murdered inside. The men were also killed as they surrounded the building in an effort to protect them.

This terrifying day was all too real for one of our partners in Rwanda. As I stood in the church, he told me how his twelve-year-old son had come there for safety that day. He narrowly escaped the tragedy by jumping out one of the windows and running to safety.

When the church reopened its doors after the genocide, 600 orphans but no adults attended. Many members of the congregation had died. Those who were left were afraid to go back to the church.

Knives, bombs, and guns were not the only weapons of the Rwandan genocide. At least 500,000 Tutsi women were systematically raped by men who knew they were HIV positive.[17] This was used as a genocidal weapon to infect as many women as possible and cause suffering and death. Hutu women married to Tutsis were also raped as a punishment.[18]

Years later, the effects of this tragedy are still being seen throughout Rwanda. By 2001, an estimated 264,000 children had lost one or both parents to AIDS.[19]

We were told that the people of Rwanda are still finding more bodies every day. As perpetrators of the genocide are released from prison, they begin to confess where more graves filled with bodies are located.

Just finding a way to bury these bodies is a monumental task. They have used large coffins, each containing the remains of about 50 people. They place 200 coffins together (10,000 people) and bury them under a huge stone block. I visited the Kigali Memorial Centre in Rwanda where a number of these coffins are buried.

As I walked through the memorial, I saw pictures of children who had been killed during the genocide. Listed were their names, their ages, what they liked about school, and what their hobbies and interests were. At the end, it told how they were killed. I could barely read the words: "smashed against a building," "macheted in mother's arms," "stabbed in eyes and head."[20] It was unimaginable. Babies, toddlers, and children coldly slaughtered!

> "We're not after charity. We're after justice!"
>
> Bono[21]

A guard with a machine gun was posted at one of the church memorial sites. I asked our partners later in the day why he was there. They explained that if he was not there, the Hutus would come and destroy the church, removing the caskets and bodies. "They don't want the world to know. They want us to forget."

As I looked at the images of one memorial, a particular quote pierced my heart. "I did not make myself an orphan."[22] The author was listed only as an unknown child affected by the genocide in Rwanda. But the child very well could have been Josianne or any of the other orphans left abandoned.

The ones who are suffering the most are the children. They are innocent. What we do will impact them more than anyone else. We should be concerned about the children and the future of Africa, not about the past. We must help the children, and that help must be more than just physical assistance. There are unbelievable emotional scars in the minds and hearts of these suffering young men and women.

Children are the future of Rwanda. According to UNICEF, more than half the population of Rwanda is under eighteen years old, and over 1 million have been left orphaned by AIDS and genocide.[23] They are struggling to pick themselves up out of tragedy and rebuild. But the need is so great in this poor, devastated country.

Maybe the response to the genocide of Rwanda was so muted because of prejudice against the people of Africa.

Maybe it is because we've seen too many images of women and children with dirty faces, dust-covered bodies, and torn clothes—images of them barefoot outside small huts, little more than skin and bones. We forget these are people who feel and hurt just like us.

Before we left Josianne's modest home in that village filled with child-led households, we stopped to take a quick picture with Josianne and her young sister. The wind was blowing my hair, and I was having trouble keeping it out of my eyes. Just like an experienced mother, Josianne reached up and gently tucked the hair behind my ears. This may sound like a small, insignificant detail, but it's something that has stuck with me and reminded me of the burden she bears. Josianne is an orphan—not by choice. And she is a mother—not by choice.

I am not sure the wrongs committed against Josianne and the people of Rwanda will ever completely be made right here on earth. Sure, most of the perpetrators have been brought to justice, but how can you ever right these kinds of wrongs? Will true justice ever really be served?

I don't know. But I do believe this: justice can come—a biblical justice that not only rights wrongs but also restores hope.

In his book *The Next Christians*, Gabe Lyons discusses the differences between Christians today and what he believes the next Christians will look like, act like, and be known for. He calls this new generation of Christians "restorers," and here is part of what he says about them:

> Restorers exhibit the mind-set, humility, and commitment that seem destined to rejuvenate the momentum of the faith. They have a peculiar way of thinking, being and doing that is radically different from previous generations. Telling others about Jesus is important, but conversion isn't their only motive. Their mission is to infuse the world with beauty, grace, justice and love.
>
> I call them restorers because they envision the world as it was meant to be and they work toward that vision. Restorers

seek to mend the earth's brokenness. They recognize that the world will not be completely healed until Christ's return, but they believe the process begins now as we partner with God. Through sowing seeds of restoration, they believe others will see Christ through us and the Christian faith will reap a much larger harvest.[24]

If justice is really all about making things right again, then justice is all about restoration.

You don't have to look far for a place to let justice roll: a hurting neighbor, a homeless man outside the grocery store, a couple going through a divorce, a friend mourning the loss of a loved one, a hungry child halfway around the world, or an entire country nearly destroyed by genocide. Opportunities for restoring hope through justice are all around us.

Unfortunately, most people of faith today are not well known for "infusing the world with beauty, grace, justice, and love"—but I am beginning to believe we can be. I want to be.

Not many of us will be faced with injustices like the genocide that happened in Rwanda. But we all face injustice every day. And how we respond shows the world who we really are and what we really believe. As people of faith who have experienced the unexplainable gift of God's grace lavished upon us, justice should be a natural outpouring from our lives. We are giving out of what has already been given to us.

Years ago I read a memorable story in one of my favorite books, *Good News about Injustice* by Gary Haugen. He describes a minister asking the congregation to imagine the story of the feeding of the five thousand in a slightly different way. Of course we know the multitude was hungry, and the disciples found a little boy with five loaves of bread and two fishes. In the original story, Jesus multiplies the food and the disciples have enough to feed the entire gathering of people.

But in this revised version of the story, the preacher asks them to imagine if the disciples just kept taking the multiplied bread and fish without passing it out to the others.

What if they just kept taking it and thanking Jesus for it? While the piles of fish and bread grow around them, they continue to say, "'Thank you, thank you, thank you, thank you, thank you, thank you, thank you, thank you!'—all the while never passing along the food to people. And then beneath the mounting piles of food, the disciples even could be heard complaining to Jesus that he wasn't doing anything about the hungry multitude."[25]

> "The only thing necessary for the triumph of evil is for good people to do nothing."
>
> Edmund Burke[26]

Gary goes on to pose the challenge, "We can say to God, '. . . Thank you for the all the power, protection, freedom and justice you have granted us.' . . . Or we can ask, 'What have you given me, Father, that I might help those who don't have power, who don't have protection, who don't have freedom, who don't have justice?'"[27]

Through the support of a World Help friend and board member, a trauma center is now reaching out to young people in Rwanda whose lives have been affected by the genocide. This center is not only providing them with a much-needed quality education but also helping them cope with the psychological needs they are experiencing and suffering from. As one of our partners said, "Education in Rwanda faces the challenge of excessive traumatized children, who in effect are soon becoming traumatized youth, who in a few years will become traumatized adults, and soon we will have a traumatized nation." Some of the young people being helped endured witnessing their parents being murdered or even raped. But their lives are starting to change, and they are beginning to see hope.

One young girl at the center said:

> We did not know what to do with all the scarring images that had stuck with us since we lost our parents, brothers, and sisters a long time ago.

I did not like the bad thoughts and images with me at all, but how could I get them out of mind since they just came? . . . I thank God for our trauma centre; I have been helped greatly. I still do get some of these images, but it's once in a while, but before I used to stay with them almost every day.

Here is the testimony of one young man:

My father and sisters with my brothers plus other relatives all died during genocide. It's only my mother, young sister, and I who survived.

I had many problems, and I had lost hope of making it in life like other friends of mine who seemed to love being alive, which I hated. But since I began attending the trauma programmes I now feel happy about being alive, and I am ready to pass national exams and join university and become a leader in my nation. I have hope once again and am looking to the future with anticipation of good things.

Hope is now being restored all over the country of Rwanda.

Early people of faith seem to have understood justice better than we do today. They were practicing "social justice" long before the term existed and before people could debate its meaning.

Sociologist Rodney Stark, author of the book *The Rise of Christianity*, did an interesting study where he listed four traits of the early Christians in the Roman Empire:

1. The early Christians practiced a high degree of morality without being judgmental. They demonstrated a lifestyle that was an attractive contrast.
2. In a time when infanticide was rampant, when pagans often left girl babies beside streams to be killed by

138

exposure or wild animals, each morning Christians took these babies into their homes.

3. When plagues hit cities, residents would flee for the relative safety of the mountains. Christians on the other hand stayed to care for the sick and dying. Eventually non-Christian writers began to ask why only Christians showed compassion.

4. In an era in which women were treated merely as property, Christians gave them dignity.[28]

The authors of *The Hope Factor* go on to share, "These actions by God's people literally changed the direction of an empire. Could they not do the same today?"[29]

I believe that they can.

It's really not about feeling guilty. It's not about feeling guilty about the house you live in, the car you drive, the nice clothes you wear, or the vacations you take. If all we do is feel guilty, we have really missed the point.

In order for justice to be served, we have to be willing to move from guilt to action. Jim Palmer says,

> You'd have to be comatose not to feel God's hurt and anger ooze from the pages of Scripture over the oppression of the weak and vulnerable. . . . I can't seem to get away from the fact that the main message of God to his people about injustice is to get off our rear ends and do something! This goes way deeper than feeling guilty about doing more; I'm trying to figure out how I got to the place where the things that break the heart of God are so marginal to mine.[30]

It is time once again for justice to roll like a mighty river. It is time for us to slow down long enough to see the world around us . . . to wake up to the real world. And it is time for us to "get off our rear ends and do something."

Justice may not always come in the legal sense, but things can be made right again. Restoration can begin. Wrongs can be made right and hope can be restored. True justice can be served.

It is no longer about handouts. It's not about guilt or charity. It's about justice, it's about compassion, and it's about change.

Let's roll.

11

Outraged, Loud, and Bold

> Don't close your eyes
> Don't close your eyes
> This is your life, are you who you want to be?
> This is your life, are you who you want to be?
> This is your life, is it everything you dreamed
>   that it would be
> When the world was younger and you had
>   everything to lose?
>
> Switchfoot[1]

A group of businessmen and women are riding up the side of a mountain in a gondola. It is unclear where they are going or why they are headed up the mountain, but it appears that they are on their way to a meeting.

About halfway up, the gondola comes to a screeching halt. The car starts swinging back and forth high above the mountain.

The people start to panic, and the women start to scream.

One man speaks up and says, "It's okay, guys—I've done a course . . . on positive thinking. Positive thought makes a positive impact." He gets the others to start saying it with him: "Positive thought makes a positive impact. Positive thought makes a positive impact."

But one man is skeptical. As he watches them panicking and chanting their mantra, he looks around and sees a green button. He pushes the button, and the gondola starts smoothly moving up the mountain again.

This Royal Bank of Scotland commercial ends with this phrase from a narrator: "Talk is no substitute for action."[2]

I wrote a lot of words to produce this book. If you have made it to this point, you have read a lot of words. Perhaps you have even discussed what you have read with someone else. But let me tell you what would be a tragedy. Let me tell you what would make this all useless: if that was all we did—write, read, and talk.

Real change requires action. There is no substitute for it.

"Let us be the ones who say we do not accept that a child dies every three seconds simply because he does not have the drugs you and I have. Let us be the ones to say that we are not satisfied that your place of birth determines your right to life. Let us be outraged, let us be loud, and let us be bold."[3]

These powerful and challenging words were spoken by an actor—Brad Pitt. Now, I don't know Brad Pitt (although I kind of wish I did), and I don't know what his beliefs are. But when I read these words, I wish that as people of faith, we felt this same way. I wish that seeing the injustices in our world would make us outraged and that we would be loud and bold about it.

As Max Lucado said, "Get ticked off. Riled up enough to respond. Righteous anger would do a world of good. Poverty is not the lack of charity, but the lack of justice."[4] But too often we just get overwhelmed by the great need.

On the morning of April 16, 2007, the worst school shooting in US history took place at Virginia Tech, only a little over an hour from where I live. Thirty-three people, including the gunman, were left dead: thirty-three sons, daughters, husbands, wives, and friends. Living that close to Blacksburg, everyone on our staff had a connection to someone who had been on campus that tragic day. There was no way to make sense of such a senseless act. Thirty-three people were dead for no reason, most of them young students whose lives had been cut terribly short.

As I lay in bed later that week pondering all of this depressing news, I picked up a book I had been wanting to read, *The Little Red Book of Wisdom*. I read the first words of the first chapter, a quote from Euripides: "No one can confidently say that they will be living tomorrow."[5]

Wow—words that aptly fit the news of the day. I read on, clinging to every word, until I reached the closing remarks of the first chapter where the author, Mark DeMoss, says:

> We are all wise to invest life's most precious commodity for the greatest return. When I die, whenever that moment comes, I hope my passing will echo the psalmist's saying, "Teach me to number my days, that I may present to you a heart of wisdom."[6]

It was all too much for one day. The honesty of those words was more than I could bear. I broke down in tears, and for a few minutes I simply could not pull myself together.

Thoughts were racing through my head. If I were to die, what would happen to the people I would leave behind—to my family, to my two precious boys? Would I have lived a good enough life? What would I have accomplished? Would I have "numbered my days"? What would my legacy be?

Stephen Covey said that you should live your life by starting with the end in mind—asking yourself what you want written on your tombstone. This is a hard question for anyone to answer. How do you really sum up your life in a few words, and what do you want those words to be?

As a cancer survivor, my dad has a powerful and inspirational mission statement for his life: "Every day, I try to live my life in such a way that I accomplish at least one thing that will outlive me and last for eternity."

What about you? How do you want to be remembered? What will your legacy be?

It has been said, "A great life includes something worth living for, maybe even worth dying for. A portion of a great life would be devoted to something bigger, greater, grander than yourself. Something that inspires you, energizes you, pulls you forward. Something that responds to your unique talent or touch and, ultimately, makes a difference in the world around you."[7]

> "How wonderful it is that nobody need wait a single minute before starting to improve the world."
> Anne Frank[8]

Years ago when World Help began our child sponsorship program, my grandmother was among our first supporters. She believed in what we were doing and wanted to help. Her goal was to recruit twenty-five child sponsors. And how did she do this? Tea parties—yes, that's right, tea parties. She hosted tea party after tea party and invited her friends to get involved until she had reached her goal.

Before I left to fly out for her funeral a couple years ago, I found a book that I remembered she had given me. It was about the life of Mother Teresa—a life that touched literally millions of people. I remembered how much I learned when I first read it. I even saw the pages I had underlined and highlighted. And tucked in between the pages was a handwritten note from my grandmother that she had sent to me along with the book in 1997.

My grandmother wrote incredible handwritten letters. I only wish I had kept more of them. In an age where email has all but replaced the art of letter writing, she was an example of how to use written words on beautiful paper to encourage someone, lift them up, and simply tell them that you love them. How I miss her letters.

This particular letter is quite special to me and one I will always cherish:

> You bring me so much happiness—just being *YOU!* How blessed I am to say you are my precious granddaughter.
>
> Your dad saw this book on my end table. I just finished it. He thought you might like to read it. Hope it gives you a great good knowledge of her ministry in India and how she was able to do so much.
>
> I pray without government officials, worldwide fame, or a strong church behind you that you will, with the compassion of Mother Teresa, build a ministry that will bring *many* into God's house and Kingdom for eternity.
>
> May you practice your "calling" "with loving availability, with wise competency, and with unforgettable humanity"—especially toward the orphans.
>
> I'm pleasured to be just a small part of it!
>
> You are always in my prayers—and always in my heart.
>
> I love you,
>
> Grammie

This letter could be one of the reasons that so many years later I am still trying to live out my "calling." No, a letter alone can't do that, but the love and prayers of a godly grandmother can certainly go a long way. What I wouldn't give to leave a legacy of "loving availability, wise competency, and unforgettable humanity."

Looking back makes you realize how quickly time passes. I have learned the importance of the decisions we make in our lives and the far-reaching effects of them. The psalmist's words are true and wise: "Teach us to number our days" (90:12 NIV).

In his book *The Traveler's Gift*, Andy Andrews says this:

> There comes a time in every person's life when a decision is required. And that decision, should you make it, will have

a far-reaching effect on generations yet unborn. There is a thin thread that weaves only from you to hundreds of thousands of lives. Your example, your actions, and yes, even one decision can literally change the world. Let me say that one more time. One decision, that *you* make, can literally change the world.[9]

As my life is flashing by, I hope that I am making decisions that will have far-reaching effects. I hope that the decisions I make each and every day will literally change the world.

Sometimes that seems like a stretch when I am doing simple, daily, menial tasks. But that is life—real, everyday life. Whether I am on the streets of Haiti, in a village in Africa, or in my kitchen making dinner for my family, I have a choice as to how I am going to live my life. I choose to number my days and make decisions that can impact the world, because I believe change is on the way, a new day is dawning, and hope is rising.

There is reason to be hopeful even in the face of such great needs. Progress is being made, and now more than ever we have reason to believe that we can see an end to the world's biggest problems in our lifetime. As Jacqueline Novogratz says in *The Blue Sweater*,

> "Speak up for the people who have no voice,
> for the rights of all the down-and-outers.
> Speak out for justice!
> Stand up for the poor and destitute!"
> Proverbs 31:8–9 Message

> There is cause for optimism. Look at the progress in the world over the past 20 years. . . . More than 300 million people have been lifted out of poverty in the past quarter century alone. . . . There is a reason to believe that people everywhere can lift themselves up, but they have to be given the tools to do so. We can only open doors so that they can walk through them. . . . We have only one world for all of us on earth, and the future really is ours to create in a world we dare to imagine together.[10]

Change does not always happen overnight. Sometimes it is ten years in the making.

I first met Rey in 2000. He was one of the children in our first international children's choir, Children of the World. I hosted him in my home during his first few weeks in America. I enjoyed getting to know this little nine-year-old-boy who had come from a life of extreme poverty in the Philippines. A child like Rey had little hope for a future. His father was in prison, and his mother was struggling to support her children and keep the family together.

I still remember when he showed me a picture of his home. My heart broke to think that he lived in such conditions. Rey was given the opportunity to travel with our choir for ten months and to be a part of our child sponsorship program. Ten years later, you can see the results. Here is a letter we recently received from Rey:

> I am really thankful that God has used somebody to help me in reaching my dreams and goals in life. I [have been] part of the sponsorship program since fourth grade and now I just graduated from college. I was able to earn a degree in Bachelor of Science in Airline Management through your help. Thank you so much for that great opportunity for me to become somebody out of nobody. I get to know you through my dad who is still in prison since I was seven years old. [Because of] your partners here in the Philippines I get to be one of the lucky kids to be sponsored and start dreaming for the future. Even though my Dad is still not with us [I am] still happy and thankful that God is there always, filling the gaps of my earthly father.
>
> We've encountered lots of challenges in life, but still we didn't gave up, for we know that God has purpose why He gave that to us. During my four years in college, challenges in school, family and personal life came in, but still I fight for what I dreamed to become someday. You also gave me the strength and courage to pursue and overcome those challenges in life. When I go up to the stage to accept my diploma, I really [can't describe] the feelings I felt. I was nervous, excited, surprised. . . . I came to realize that this is it! This is

the day. The day that I've been waiting for. The day that I'll be entering into the real world.

Words are not really enough in expressing my gratitude and joy of your help. Without you, I would perhaps be still nobody. . . . Thank you so much for the help. I will never forget and you will be in my heart forever. I love you guys![11]

Real change does not usually happen overnight—but it is worth the wait.

Thousands of children were left orphaned at the end of the Korean War. After seeing these suffering children, Robert Pierce, founder of World Vision and Samaritan's Purse, made the now famous statement, "Let my heart be broken with the things that break the heart of God."[12]

Over the years my dad has challenged me to pray that special prayer on every trip I have been on: "Break my heart with the things that break the heart of God." God has never failed to answer this prayer in my life, time and time again. Hungry children, homeless families, abandoned babies . . . he has used them all to break my heart.

He has also used them to make me pray a new prayer—or perhaps I should say to answer my own prayer.

Looking at the needs of the world, we can so easily get overwhelmed. We want to cry out to God and ask, "Why do you allow this to happen? Why do you allow children to die because they have no food, water, or medicine? Why do you allow young girls to be abused and sold into slavery? Why do you allow people to get sick and die simply because they don't have something as basic as clean water?"

But I often wonder if God is calmly but sternly responding back by saying, "Why do *you* allow this to happen?"

You see, I believe that God in all his mystery has chosen to use us to meet the needs of the world. He does not have another plan—that is it. And even though I don't completely understand it, I do believe it! Shane Claiborne says in his book *Becoming the Answer to Our Prayers,*

> That's the beautiful mystery: we have a God who chooses to need us. We have a God who doesn't want to change the world without us. We have a God who longs to cooperate with us, to allow us to fail and flounder and who promises to make up for our shortcomings, but nonetheless wants us. It's the story of our faith. . . .
>
> So when we see a problem like the starving masses, is the answer God or is the answer us? We think Jesus would answer YES. The answer is both.[13]

Doing a world of good is oftentimes just doing what you already know how to do . . . like making a T-shirt.

Twenty-year-old college students Marianna and Gillian have been friends for years. At seventeen, they made the commitment to begin sponsoring children. "The Lord says to take care of widows and orphans, and I realized I hadn't been doing that," Marianna remembers. They started sponsoring one child, and now they sponsor eight. But sponsoring eight children for a year comes to nearly $3,000. How is that even possible for two college students?

A textile design major, Marianna put her love to work, creating her own unique brand. She started designing customized, handmade T-shirts for her friends, and now their business has grown to become the main funding source for their sponsorships. Marianna hopes to someday bring her skills to Southeast Asia, teaching victims of sex trafficking to sew so they can escape the sex industry. Gillian also has dreams of using her degree in social work to work with refugees, possibly in Uganda, where she had the opportunity to study abroad.

Remarkably, on a World Help trip for college students, Marianna and Gillian were able to meet one of their sponsored children from Uganda, a girl named Ketty. "Talking to Ketty about her life makes it real to us," Gillian explains.

"Forming authentic relationships and having meaningful communication has been really impactful."

It all started with a needle, thread, and a passion to make a difference in one child's life.

"Our lives begin to end the day we become silent about things that matter."

Martin Luther King Jr.[14]

What is your "T-shirt"? Do you see a problem or need that is waiting to be addressed? There's no skill, passion, or dream too small or insignificant. You're not too old or too young; you're not too busy or too limited; and you're never too late. There's never been a better time than now.

In a graduation address, Bill Gates told the students:

"As you leave Harvard, you have technology that members of my class never had. You have awareness of global inequity, which we did not have . . . And I hope you will come back here to Harvard thirty years from now and reflect on what you have done with your talent and your energy. I hope you will judge yourselves not on your professional accomplishments alone, but also on how well you have addressed the world's deepest inequities . . . on how well you treated people a world away who have nothing in common with you but their humanity.[15]

Tom Brokaw once said, "You are educated. Your certification is in your degree. You may think of it as the ticket to the good life. Let me ask you to think of an alternative. Think of it as your ticket to change the world."[16]

We each have a ticket to change the world. Some of us have time. Some of us have resources. Some have networks of influence. Others have great passion. But we each have a ticket. The question is, what will you do with yours?

Do you want to simply live a life of convenience? Safety? Security? When you come to the end of the only life you will ever have, do you want to look back on a life filled with shopping, golfing, and vacations to exotic places? A life filled with insecurity and obsession over how you look and whether you are good enough? A life spent trying to measure up to what you have been told is the American dream?

A few years ago an incredible movie about an unstoppable man was released. The movie was called *Amazing Grace*, and the man was William Wilberforce. I am sure you know his story. The tireless work of Wilberforce led to the Abolition Act of 1833 which abolished slavery in most of the British Empire.

There is a scene at the end of the movie that I have not been able to forget. Right after the announcement has been made that the bill to abolish the slave trade has passed, and as the thunderous applause begins to fade in the House of Commons, Lord Charles Fox stands and says these powerful words: "When people speak of great men, they think of men like Napoleon—men of violence. Rarely do they think of peaceful men. But contrast the reception they will receive when they return home from their battles. Napoleon will arrive in pomp and in power—a man who has achieved the very summit of earthly ambition. And yet his dreams will be haunted by the oppressions of war. William Wilberforce, however, will return to his family, lay his head on his pillow, and remember the slave trade is no more."[17]

When you lay your head on your pillow at night, what do you want to dream about? What do you want to rest knowing?

Tonight, when I lay my head down, unfortunately I will not be able to say that poverty is no more. I will not be able to say that children are not suffering. I will not be able to say that true justice has come.

But I will be able to rest. I will rest knowing that I have been able to help save one life. And tomorrow I will lie down being able to say that I helped save another life. I will dream of Rey, Nildo, Margarita, Jamira, Josianne, and the countless others who have touched my life. And I will remember that we can do a world of good, one person at a time.

As Bono sings, "Every generation has a chance to change the world."[18] Our time is now.

So I want to challenge you: from now on, when you see the injustices in our world, be outraged, be loud, and be bold. Live a life fully awake to the needs of the world. Let God break your heart—and then when he does, let him use you to change the world.

12

Do Good Now

Inspiration is when your heart and soul get moved to the point of action.

Anonymous

I never intended to write a "how-to" book or leave you with "ten steps to changing the world." That seems way too clichéd and much too impersonal. Yet what would be worse would be for you to read this book and do nothing.

How you choose to get involved is up to you. But in case you're stuck and need a push, here are a few ideas for things we can all be doing—little things that can do a world of good.

Discover

Find your passion. We each have one. Discover what you're passionate about and educate yourself about that issue. Maybe it is children, water, hunger, extreme poverty, or trafficking and slavery.

What wrecks you and disturbs you the most? Find it and then become an expert on it. You can use your knowledge to be a voice for your cause.

Fight

Once you know what you are passionate about—fight for it. Join advocacy groups like ONE.org and use your voice to draw attention to the great needs facing our world today. Recently ONE members used their voice to urge Congress to dedicate funds to provide vaccinations that will save 4 million lives in the next five years. That's pretty incredible work—and all you have to do is use your voice.

Activism is not a bad word, and it is exactly what we need. Become an activist for your cause.

Invest

Invest in the life of a child and especially in the life of a young girl. Just about everyone has heard of child sponsorship. Maybe we have grown a little calloused to it because it is talked about so much and we see commercials on TV and pop-up ads on our computer screens about it every day. But I still believe this is one of the most effective ways to change a child's life. For more information and to begin your special relationship with a child in need, visit www.worldhelp.net/sponsor.

Drill

You have the power today to literally save a life. On average, just $15 can give one person access to clean water.

Cause*life* is a movement of people dedicated to providing the most essential need for human life—clean water. The mission of cause*life* is to provide clean water to those in need in developing countries. By raising global awareness, involving passionate activists and volunteers, and implementing practical clean water solutions, cause*life* works to bring clean water that changes lives and transforms communities.

Visit www.causelife.org today for more information and to see how you can join the movement.

Experience

There is really no substitute for actually going and seeing these needs firsthand. I am convinced that it not only changes the lives of those you touch but will forever change your life as well.

There are many opportunities out there to "go" and many opportunities to serve. I would love nothing more than to go on that journey with you. Visit www.noelyeatts.com for more information and to sign up to join me for a life-changing experience.

My hope and prayer is that this book has left you truly "awake" to the needs of the world and ready to make a difference. Let's go out and do a world of good right now!

Acknowledgments

Pat—Thank you for never holding me back and for believing in me even when I don't believe in myself. Your sense of justice and true compassion inspire me every day.

Riley and Bentley—Thank you for giving up a little bit of your mom so that this project could become a reality. I'm so proud that you are already living your lives awake to the needs of the world. I love you both more than you know.

Dad—You taught me everything I know. Thank you for opening my eyes at such an early age and for sharing your passion with me. It was contagious.

Mom—You have always been my biggest cheerleader. No matter what new thing I decided to try, you made me believe I could do it. I hope to be that kind of mom.

Christa—You are so much more than an assistant . . . you are my friend. Without you, this book would have never seen the light of day. I can't thank you enough for your hours of hard work and research. Thank you for sharing my passion. We did it!

The World Help staff—If you're going to try to change the world, you might as well do it with people you love! I couldn't be more proud to work with such a dedicated group of people. Thank you for believing that what we do is so much more than a job.

Donna—You inspired me when I was young, and you were there when I believe my eyes first started to open to the world around me. I will be forever grateful for the influence you had on my life.

David Van Diest—Thank you for giving me the opportunity to tell my story and share my passion.

There are no words great enough to express my gratitude to God for his unending love and grace. Thank you for allowing me to play a small part in your vision to restore hope to a hurting world.

And to the children around the world who continue to inspire and challenge me—thank you. May hope arrive soon.

Notes

Introduction

1. Bono, *On the Move* (Nashville: W Publishing Group, 2006), 29.

2. Dan Zadra and Kobi Yamada, *1: How Many People Does It Take to Make a Difference?* (Seattle: Compendium, 2010), 9.

3. Timothy Keller, *Generous Justice: How God's Grace Makes Us Just* (New York: Penguin Group, 2010), 107.

Chapter 1 The Lucky One

1. "ADL Honors Polish Women Who Sheltered Jews During the Holocaust," Anti-Defamation League, February 14, 2011, http://www.adl.org/NR/exeres/88F2B416-58F2-4BC4-9052-937CC6E271D0,0B1623CA-D5A4-465D-A369-DF6E8679CD9E,frameless.htm.

2. "Poverty in Guatemala," Poverty Central, October 6, 2010, http://www.thepovertycentral.com/view/99756/Poverty_In_Guatemala.

3. "Central America and Caribbean: Guatemala," Central Intelligence Agency, June 14, 2011, https://www.cia.gov/library/publications/the-world-factbook/geos/gt.html.

4. Augusto Zimmermann, "Welcome to Brazil, a Paradise of Impunity for All Kinds of Criminals," *Brazzil*, February 22, 2008, http://www.brazzil.com/articles/188-february-2008/10042.html.

5. Hannah Elliott, "NBC Nightly News to Feature American Baptist Ministry," Associated Baptist Press, December 21, 2006, http://www.abpnews.com/index.php?option=com_content&task=view&id=1697&Itemid=118.

6. John Cook, *The Book of Positive Quotations*, ed. Steve Deger and Leslie Ann Gibson (Minneapolis: Fairview Press, 1997), 473.

7. "Quotes on Compassion," Charter for Compassion, accessed January 2, 2012, http://charterforcompassion.org.pk/learn.html.

8. "Mother Teresa of Calcutta Quotes," ThinkExist.com, October 27, 2001, http://thinkexist.com/quotation/i_know_god_will_not_give_me_anything_i_cant/9211.html.

9. Paul Slovic, "Numbed by Numbers," *Foreign Policy*, March 13, 2007, http://www.foreignpolicy.com/articles/2007/03/12/numbed_by_numbers.

Chapter 2 Comfortably Numb

1. "Famous Quotes about Children," Compassion, accessed January 2, 2012, http://www.compassion.com/child-advocacy/find-your-voice/famous-quotes/default.htm.

2. "Political Declaration on HIV/AIDS: Intensifying our Efforts to Eliminate HIV/AIDS," Resolution Adopted by the General Assembly on June 10, 2011, United Nations, http://www.unaids.org/en/media/unaids/contentassets/documents/document/2011/06/20110610_UN_A-RES-65-277_en.pdf.

3. Tetsunao Yamamori, David Dageforde, and Tina Bruner, eds., *The Hope Factor: Engaging the Church in the HIV/AIDS Crisis* (Waynesboro, GA: Authentic and World Vision, 2003), xi.

4. "Service-Learning Resources," Aquinas College, accessed on June 30, 2010, http://www.aquinas.edu/servicelearning/resources.html.

5. Anderson Cooper, *Dispatches from the Edge: A Memoir of War, Disasters, and Survival* (New York: HarperCollins, 2006), 8.

6. Alexander Irwin, Joyce Millen, and Dorothy Fallows, "Global AIDS: Myths and Facts—Tools for Fighting the AIDS Pandemic," American Medical Student Association (AMSA), 2010, http://www.amsa.org/AMSA/Homepage/About/Committees/Global/MythsFacts.aspx.

7. *Global Report: UNAIDS Report on the Global AIDS Epidemic 2010*, Joint United Nations Programme on HIV/AIDS (UNAIDS), 112, http://www.unaids.org/globalreport/documents/20101123_GlobalReport_full_en.pdf.

8. "Mother Teresa Quotes," Inspirational Quotes Change Lives, 2011, http://www.inspirational-quotes-change-lives.com/motherteresaquotes.html.

9. Bill Hybels, *Holy Discontent: Fueling the Fire That Ignites Personal Vision* (Grand Rapids: Zondervan, 2007).

10. John Stott, *Culture and the Bible* (Downers Grove: InterVarsity, 1981), 36; also available online at www.intervarsity.org/ism/article/1952.

Chapter 3 Eyes Glued Shut

1. Sara Groves, "I Saw What I Saw," *Tell Me What You Know*, © 2007 Sara Groves Music (admin. by Music Services). All rights reserved. ASCAP.

2. "Quotes on Participation," Anti-Defamation League, 2011, http://www.adl.org/education/holocaust/quotations.pdf.

3. Vijayendra Mohanty, "The Meaning of 'I See You' in Avatar," Vijayendra Mohanty—Storyteller, December 23, 2009, http://www.vmohanty.com/2009/the-meaning-of-i-see-you-in-avatar/.

4. Jay Michaelson, "The Meaning of Avatar: Everything Is God (A Response to Ross Douthat and Other Naysayers of 'Pantheism')," *Huffington Post*, December

22, 2009, http://www.huffingtonpost.com/jay-michaelson/the-meaning-of-avatar-eve_b_400912.html.

5. Associated Press, "Despite Tensions, Tourists Flock to Korean DMZ: Hundreds Visit Front Lines Weekly to Glimpse Across Last Cold War Frontier," MSNBC.com, November 4, 2006, http://www.msnbc.msn.com/id/15563058/ns/travel-destination_travel/t/despite-tensions-tourists-flock-korean-dmz/.

6. "Country Profiles," Open Doors, 2011, http://www.opendoors.org.au/persecutedchristians/countryprofiles/.

7. "Roots of the Crisis," Enough: The Project to End Genocide and Crimes Against Humanity, 2011, http://www.enoughproject.org/files/pdf/crisis_roots_uganda.pdf.

8. Jeevan Vasagar, "The Nightwalkers," The Guardian, February 10, 2006, http://www.guardian.co.uk/world/2006/feb/10/uganda.jeevanvasagar.

9. "Uganda: Difficulties Continue for Returnees and Remaining IDPs as Development Phase Begins," Internal Displacement Monitoring Centre, December 28, 2010, http://www.internal-displacement.org/countries/Uganda.

10. "About," Tronie Foundation, 2010, http://www.troniefoundation.org/about.html.

11. Chuck Neubauer, "Human Bondage Hits US Heartland: Illicit Trade for Labor, Sex Generates Billions in Profits," Washington Times, March 27, 2011, http://www.washingtontimes.com/news/2011/mar/27/human-bondage-hits-us-heartland/print/.

12. "Child Protection from Violence, Exploitation, and Abuse—UNICEF in Action," UNICEF, October 11, 2010, http://www.unicef.org/protection/index_action.html.

13. Neubauer, "Human Bondage Hits US Heartland."

14. Amanda Kloer, "Ten Times More Slaves Now Than at Peak of Trans-Atlantic Trade," Change.org, October 12, 2009, http://news.change.org/stories/ten-times-more-slaves-now-than-at-peak-of-trans-atlantic-trade.

15. "Gandhi's Vision and Ground Realities," Mahatma Gandhi, accessed December 19, 2011, http://www.mkgandhi.org/articles/gandhi_vision.htm.

16. Wikipedia, s.v. "Debbie Downer," June 21, 2011, http://en.wikipedia.org/wiki/Debbie_Downer.

17. "Marian Wright Edelman," Architects of Peace Foundation, accessed December 13, 2011, http://www.architectsofpeace.org/architects-of-peace/marian-wright-edelman.

18. Ravi Zacharias, Deliver Us From Evil (Nashville: Thomas Nelson, 1998), 175.

19. Jim Palmer, Divine Nobodies: Shedding Religion to Find God (Nashville: Thomas Nelson, 2006), 144.

20. "Laugh Quotes," Winning Solutions, 2011, http://www.winning-solutions.com/LaughQuotes.html.

21. Personal correspondence. Used by permission.

22. Gary Haugen, Terrify No More (Nashville: Thomas Nelson, 2005), ix.

Chapter 4 The Meaning of Enough

1. Matthew West, "My Own Little World," The Story of Your Life, © 2005 Alfred Music Publishing.

2. "Extreme Poverty, HIV/AIDS, Slavery and Broken Communities: Our Generation's Responsibility," One%Matters, accessed on January 2, 2012, http://www.one percentmatters.org.

3. Institute in Basic Youth Conflicts, *The Pineapple Story: A Humorous Yet Profound True Story* (Oak Brook, IL: Institute in Basic Youth Conflicts, 1978), 22.

4. Ibid.

5. Max Lucado, *Outlive Your Life: You Were Made to Make a Difference* (Nashville: Thomas Nelson, 2010), 103.

6. James Davies, Susanna Sandström, Anthony Shorrocks, and Edward Wolff, "The World Distribution of Household Wealth," United Nations University: World Institution for Development Economic Research, February 2008, http://www.wider. unu.edu/publications/working-papers/discussion-papers/2008/en_GB/dp2008-03/_files/78918010772127840/default/dp2008-03.pdf, 11.

7. Ibid., 7.

8. Wess Stafford, *Too Small to Ignore: Why Children Are the Next Big Thing* (Colorado Springs: WaterBrook Press, 2005), 175.

9. "Global Hunger Declining, But Still Unacceptably High: International Hunger Targets Difficult to Reach," Food and Agriculture Organization of the United Nations, September 2010, http://www.fao.org/docrep/012/al390e/al390e00.pdf.

10. "Millennium Development Goals: Progress towards the Health-Related Millennium Development Goals," World Health Organization (WHO), May 2011, http://www.who.int/mediacentre/factsheets/fs290/en/index.html.

11. "New Data Show 1.4 Billion Live on Less Than US $1.25 a Day, But Progress Against Poverty Remains Strong," The World Bank, August 26, 2008, http://go.worldbank.org/F9ZJUH97T0.

12. Gilmore Foundation, 2006, http://gilmorefoundation.org/childrens_initia tive.htm.

13. Peter Singer, *The Life You Can Save* (New York: Random House, 2009), 8.

14. Robert Rector and Rachel Sheffield, "Understanding Poverty in the United States: Surprising Facts About America's Poor," The Heritage Foundation, September 13, 2011, http://www.heritage.org/research/reports/2011/09/understanding-poverty-in-the-united-states-surprising-facts-about-americas-poor.

15. "World Summit for Social Development Programme of Action: Chapter 2—Eradication of Poverty," United Nations, August 21, 2000, http://www.un.org/esa/socdev/wssd/text-version/agreements/poach2.htm.

16. "Women in Mature Economies Control Household Spending," Marketing Charts, May 18, 2010, http://www.marketingcharts.com/topics/asia-pacific/women-in-mature-economies-control-household-spending-12931/.

17. "The Average American Woman . . . ," Gather, February 3, 2008, http://www.gather.com/viewArticle.action?articleId=281474977247969.

18. "Bertrand Russell Quotes," Essential Life Skills, accessed on January 2, 2012, http://www.essentiallifeskills.net/bertrand-russell-quotes.html.

19. Susan Hunter, *Black Death: AIDS in Africa* (New York: Palgrave MacMillan, 2003), 28.

20. Luis Bush, *Raising Up a New Generation from the 4/14 Window to Transform the World* (Flushing, NY: Transform World New Generation, 2009), 17.

21. Shane Claiborne, *The Irresistible Revolution: Living as an Ordinary Radical* (Grand Rapids: Zondervan, 2006), 51.

22. "The Poverty and Justice Bible," World Vision Resources, accessed on December 21, 2011, http://www.worldvisionresources.com/poverty-justice-bible-p-376.html.

23. Claiborne, *Irresistible Revolution*, 164–165.

24. "Poverty Around the World," Global Issues, November 12, 2011, http://www.globalissues.org/article/4/poverty-around-the-world.

25. "About MDGs: What They Are," Millennium Development Project, 2006, http://www.unmillenniumproject.org/goals/index.htm.

26. "We Can End Poverty, 2015: Millennium Development Goals," United Nations Summit, September 20–22, 2010, http://www.un.org/millenniumgoals/pdf/MDG_FS_1_EN.pdf.

27. Jacqueline Novogratz, *The Blue Sweater: Bridging the Gap Between Rich and Poor in an Interconnected World* (New York: Rodale, 2009), 102.

28. "A 10 Minute Guide: Poverty," World Vision UK, 2009, http://www.worldvision.org.uk/upload/pdf/10_min_Poverty.pdf.

29. Ash Barker, *Make Poverty Personal: Taking the Poor as Seriously as the Bible Does* (Grand Rapids: Baker Books, 2009), 11.

Chapter 5 I Knew You Would Come

1. Coldplay, "A Message," *X&Y*, words and music by Guy Berrman, Will Champion, Chris Martin, and Jon Buckland, copyright © 2005 by Universal Music Publishing, MGB Ltd. All rights in the United States administered by Universal Music—MGB Songs. International copyright secured. All rights reserved. Reprinted by permission of Hal Leonard Corporation.

2. "Inhumane Conditions for Romanian Lost Generation," *20/20*, accessed June 30, 2011, http://abcnews.go.com/2020/story?id=124078&page=1.

3. "Take Action Heroes," Purpose Driven Connection, March 9, 2009, http://www.purposedriven.com/article.html?c=123732&l=1.

4. "Our Values," Wings of Peace International, accessed on January 2, 2012, https://www.wingsofpeaceinternational.org/about-our-values.php.

5. "Guatemala Overview—Malnutrition," UNICEF, October 4, 2010, http://www.unicef.org/guatemala/english/overview_18012.htm.

6. Henri Nouwen, *Compassion*, quoted in Shayne Moore, *Global Soccer Mom* (Grand Rapids: Zondervan, 2011), 6.

Chapter 6 The Ripple Effect

1. OFED International, accessed on January 2, 2012, http://www.ofedinternational.org.

2. Quoted in Nicholas Kristof and Sheryl WuDunn, *Half the Sky: Turning Oppression into Opportunity for Women Worldwide* (New York: Random House, 2009), xi.

3. Jessica Laufer, "How Collaboration Leads to Opportunity," *Investing in Women and Girls*, no. 2 (2011): 4.

4. UNIFEM, "Gender Justice: Key to Achieving the Millennium Development Goals," United Nations Girls' Education Initiative, December, 2010, http://www.ungei.org/resources/index_2648.html.

5. Kata Fustos, "Despite Wide-Ranging Benefits, Girls' Education and Empowerment Overlooked in Developing Countries," Population Reference Bureau, April, 2010, http://www.prb.org/Articles/2010/girlseducation.aspx.

6. "Ending Poverty—Why Empower Women and Girls?," CARE, accessed June 29, 2011, http://www.care.org/getinvolved/advocacy/pdfs/whyempowerwomen.pdf.

7. Hunter, Black Death, 22.

8. "Political Declaration on HIV/AIDS: Intensifying our Efforts to Eliminate HIV/AIDS," Resolution Adopted by the General Assembly on June 10, 2011, United Nations, http://www.unaids.org/en/media/unaids/contentassets/documents/document/2011/06/20110610_UN_A-RES-65-277_en.pdf.

9. Alexander Irwin, Joyce Millen, and Dorothy Fallows, "Global AIDS: Myths and Facts—Tools for Fighting the AIDS Pandemic," American Medical Student Association (AMSA), 2010, http://www.amsa.org/AMSA/Homepage/About/Committees/Global/MythsFacts.aspx.

10. Ruth Levine, Cynthia Lloyd, Margaret Greene, and Caren Grown, "Girls Count: A Global Investment and Action Agenda," Coalition for Adolescent Girls, 2009, http://www.coalitionforadolescentgirls.org/sites/default/files/Girls_Count_2009.pdf, 52.

11. Nirit Ben-Ari and Ernest Harsch, "Sexual Violence, an 'Invisible War Crime': Sierra Leone Truth Commission Condemns Abuse, Discrimination," Africa Renewal 18, no. 4 (January 2005): 1. Available online at http://www.un.org/ecosocdev/geninfo/afrec/vol18no4/184sierraleone.htm.

12. Kristof and WuDunn, Half the Sky, 83.

13. "Ending Violence Against Women," UN Women National Committee UK, accessed on June 30, 2011, http://www.unwomenuk.org/about-us/strategic-goal-2/.

14. Claudia Feldman, "New York Times Columnist Nicholas Kristof to Appear at Rice University," Houston Chronicle, October 16, 2009, http://www.chron.com/disp/story.mpl/life/books/6671087.html.

15. Francisca de Haan, "A Brief Survey of Women's Rights," UN Chronicle, February 25, 2010, http://www.un.org/wcm/content/site/chronicle/cache/bypass/home/archive/issues2010/empoweringwomen/briefsurveywomensrights.

16. Kristof and WuDunn, Half the Sky, xvii.

17. "Trafficking in Persons," US Department of State, June 2005, http://www.state.gov/documents/organization/47255.pdf, 7.

18. Chuck Neubauer, "Human Bondage Hits US Heartland."

19. "Human Trafficking," Rescue Foundation, accessed on June 30, 2011, http://www.rescuefoundation.net/human-traffic.html.

20. "Human Trafficking Facts and Stats," Fashion 4 Compassion, accessed January 22, 2012, http://fashion4.org/slavery/facts.asp.

21. Mary Robinson, "Marriage vs. Pregnancy: Reasons Why School-Age Girls Stop Attending School," Investing in Women and Girls, no. 2 (2011): 14.

22. "Beijing + 15: Bringing Girls into Focus," UNICEF, March 2010, http://www.unicef.org/gender/files/Beijing_plus_15_Bringing_Girls_Into_Focus_2010.pdf, 6.

23. "Working Against the Oppression of Women Around the World," Women's Rights Worldwide, 2007, http://womensrightsworldwide.org/.

24. "The State of the World's Children: Maternal and Newborn Health," UNICEF, 2009, http://www.unicef.org/sowc09/docs/SOWC09-FullReport-EN.pdf.

25. "When Pregnancy Harms," UNFPA, May 18, 2010, http://www.unfpa.org/webdav/site/global/shared/safemotherhood/docs/fistula_factsheet_en.pdf, 1.

26. Yanina Manolova, "10 Facts on Obstetric Fistula," World Health Organization, March 2010, http://www.who.int/features/factfiles/obstetric_fistula/facts/en/index2.html.

27. "What Is Fistula?" Healing Hands of Joy, 2011, http://www.healinghandsofjoy.com/index.php?option=com_content&view=article&id=22&Itemid=27.

28. UNIFEM, "Gender Justice: Key to Achieving the Millennium Development Goals," 6.

29. "Working Against the Oppression of Women Around the World," Women's Rights Worldwide, 2007, http://womensrightsworldwide.org/.

30. "Change Starts with a Collective Responsibility," *Investing in Women and Girls*, no. 2 (2011): 6.

31. "The Power of Girls' Education," UN Environment Programme, July 30, 2007, http://www.unep.org/training/programmes/Instructor%20Version/Part_2/Activities/Dimensions_of_Human_Well-Being/Education/Core%20Readings/Power_of_Girls_Education.pdf.

32. "Promises Broken: An Assessment of Children's Rights on the 10th Anniversary of the Convention on the Rights of the Children," Human Rights Watch, November 1, 1999, http://www.hrw.org/legacy/press/1999/nov/children.htm.

33. "WASH: Facts and Figures," WATSAN Resource Centre, January 20, 2006, http://www.watsanuganda.watsan.net/page/280.

34. Levine, et al, "Girls Count," 35.

35. Women's Rights World, 2011, http://womensrightsworld.com/women-quotes-womens-rights.html.

36. "Girls Determined to Get an Education," Department for International Development, accessed on December 17, 2011, http://www.dfid.gov.uk/Stories/Case-Studies/2011/Girls-determination-to-get-an-education/.

37. "What We Do," Camfed USA, accessed on June 30, 2011, http://us.camfed.org/site/PageServer?pagename=what_index.

38. Ibid.

39. "Adolescent Girls' Education," *Investing in Women and Girls*, no. 2 (2011): 8.

40. "Education Is the Most Powerful Weapon to Change the World," NGO Pulse, August 12, 2009, http://www.ngopulse.org/article/education-most-powerful-weapon-change-world.

41. Gillian Gaynair, "Invest in a Woman—Grow an Economy," *Investing in Women and Girls*, no. 2 (2011): 16.

42. *Because I Am a Girl: The State of the World's Girls*, Plan International, 2009, http://plan-international.org/files/global/publications/campaigns/BIAAG%202009.pdf, 16.

43. Ibid., 14.

44. Kristof and WuDunn, *Half the Sky*, xiv.

45. Palmer, *Divine Nobodies*, 147.

46. Shannon Galpin, "An Army of Women," *Investing in Women and Girls*, no. 2 (2011): 2.

47. "Part 4—Citizen Participation," United Nations Development Programme, April 25, 2010, http://www.undp.org.fj/index.php?option=com_news&Itemid=45 &task=view&id=175.

Chapter 7 Crystal Clear

1. "Oscilloscope Brings the Award-Winning Water Documentary *Flow: For Love of Water*," Environmental News Network, December 2, 2008, http://www.enn.com/press_releases/2737.

2. "Hurry Up in the Toilet: 2.4 Billion are Waiting," World Health Organization, 2004, http://www.who.int/ceh/publications/05sanitation.pdf.

3. "Wet and Wonderful: World Water Day," National Geographic, March 22, 2007, http://www.nationalgeographic.com/adventure/news/world-water-day.html.

4. "Poverty Biggest Enemy of Health in Developing World, Secretary-General Tells World Health Assembly," Geneva, Switzerland, May 17, 2001, http://www.un.org/News/Press/docs/2001/sgsm7808.doc.htm.

5. Water and Poverty: What's the Connection?" World Bank, March 21, 2011, http://www.youthink.worldbank.org/issues/environment/water-and-poverty-whats -the-connection.

6. Kevin Watkins, "Clean Water Is a Right But It Also Needs to Have a Price," Human Development Reports, November 10, 2006, http://hdr.undp.org/en/reports/ global/hdr2006/news/title,199,en.html.

7. "Goals, Targets and Indicators," Millennium Project, 2006, http://unmil lenniumproject.org/goals/gti.htm.

8. "Human Development Report 2006—Beyond Scarcity: Power, Poverty and the Global Water Crisis," UN Development Programme, 2006, http://hdr.undp. org/en/media/HDR06-complete.pdf, 4.

9. Jessica Berman, "WHO: Waterborne Disease Is World's Leading Killer," Voice of America News, March 17, 2005, http://www.voanews.com/english/news/a-13-2005-03-17-voa34-67381152.html.

10. "Take Action," Food and Water Watch, http://action.foodandwaterwatch. org/campaign.jsp?campaign_KEY=26890.

11. "Goal: Reduce Child Mortality," UNICEF, October 4, 2010, http://www. unicef.org/mdg/childmortality.html.

12. "Bacteria," Science Clarified, 2011, http://www.scienceclarified.com/As-Bi/ Bacteria.html.

13. "Child Survival Fact Sheet: Water and Sanitation," UNICEF, October 4, 2010, http://www.unicef.org/media/media_21423.html.

14. Andrea Gerlin, "A Simple Solution," *Time*, October 8, 2006, http://www. time.com/time/magazine/article/0,9171,1543876,00.html.

15. Anne Bragnetta, "Drawing the Connection between Malnutrition and Lack of Safe Drinking Water in Guatemala," accessed January 22, 2012, http://www .livingwatersfortheworld.org/docs/EDU_drawing-the-connection-en.doc.

16. "Malaria Facts," Center for Disease Control and Prevention, February 8, 2010, http://www.cdc.gov/malaria/about/facts.html.

17. "Water, Sanitation and Hygiene Links to Health: Facts and Figures," World Health Organization, November 2004, http://www.who.int/water_sanitation_health/factsfigures2005.pdf.

18. "Common Water and Sanitation-Related Diseases," UNICEF, April 1, 2005, http://www.unicef.org/wash/index_wes_related.html.

19. Ibid.

20. "Blinding Disease," Worldmapper, 2006, http://www.worldmapper.org/posters/worldmapper_map234_ver5.pdf.

21. Bridgette See, "De-Worming Project Frees Children From Parasitic Worms," UNICEF, November 17, 2005, http://www.unicef.org/infobycountry/Timorleste_29930.html.

22. "Background Paper on Vaccinations Against Typhoid Fever Using New-Generation Vaccines," World Health Organization, November 2007, www.who.int/entity/immunization/SAGE_Background_publicpaper_typhoid_newVaccines.pdf, 3.

23. "Typhoid and Paratyphoid Fever," Patient, accessed December 17, 2011, http://www.patient.co.uk/doctor/Typhoid-and-Paratyphoid-Fever.htm.

24. "Cholera: Mechanism for Control and Prevention," World Health Organization, May 24, 2011, http://www.who.int/cholera/technical/Resolution_Cholera A64_R15-en.pdf, 1.

25. "Cholera Deaths," Worldmapper, 2004, http://www.worldmapper.org/display.php?selected=232.

26. "Haiti's Continuing Cholera Outbreak," New York Times, May 10, 2011, http://www.nytimes.com/2011/05/11/opinion/11wed3.html.

27. United Nations Development Programme, "Beyond Scarcity: Power, Poverty and the Global Water Crisis," 2006, http://hdr.undp.org/en/media/HDR06-complete.pdf.

28. "Americans Plan to Spend Same on Christmas 2011 as in 2010," Gallup, October 20, 2011, http://www.gallup.com/poll/150203/americans-plan-spend-christmas-2011-2010.aspx.

29. "Dying for a Drink of Water," Washington Post, September 20, 2005, http://www.washingtonpost.com/wp-dyn/content/article/2005/09/19/AR2005091901295.html.

30. "Water," Changing the Present, 2010, http://www.changingthepresent.org/water/quotes.

31. Water For People, 2011, http://www.usbg.gov/education/events/loader.cfm?csModule=security/getfile&pageid=29110.

32. Singer, The Life You Can Save, 3–4.

33. "Water Facts and Figures," Rehydrate Project, 2010, http://rehydrate.org/water/index.html.

34. Rep. Earl Blumenauer, "Safe Drinking Water: Giving Life, Health, and Hope," Huffington Post, December 13, 2011, http://www.huffingtonpost.com/rep-earl-blumenauer/safe-drinking-water-givin_b_1147101.html.

35. Personal correspondence. Used by permission.

36. Irena Salina, FLOW: How Did a Handful of Corporations Steal Our Water? (New York: Oscilloscope Laboratories, 2008).

Chapter 8 Saving a Dead Man

1. "It's Bono on Line One," *Vanity Fair*, July 2007, 52.
2. "The Meaning of Compassion," Compassion International, 2011, http://www.compassion.com/child-development/meaning-of-compassion/default.htm.
3. Nina Munk, "Jeffrey Sachs's $200 Billion Dream," *Vanity Fair*, July 2007, 141.
4. Moore, *Global Soccer Mom*, 12–13.
5. Christian Buckley and Ryan Dobson, *Humanitarian Jesus: Social Justice and the Cross* (Chicago: Moody Publishers, 2010), 21.
6. "Famous Quotes about Children," Compassion, accessed January 2, 2012, http://www.compassion.com/child-advocacy/find-your-voice/famous-quotes/default.htm.
7. Gabe Lyons, *The Next Christians: The Good News About the End of Christian America* (Grand Rapids: Zondervan, 2010), 196.
8. Jim Collins and Jerry Porras, *Built to Last: Successful Habits of Visionary Companies* (New York: HarperCollins, 1997), 43–44.
9. Buckley and Dobson, *Humanitarian Jesus*, 122.
10. Lucado, *Outlive Your Life*, 107.

Chapter 9 Boring, Safe, or Significant

1. Chuck Swindoll, *Come Before Winter and Share My Hope* (Portland, OR: Multnomah, 1994), 103.
2. Martin Luther King Jr., *Strength to Love* (Minneapolis: Fortress Press, 1981), 34.
3. Thomas Berman, "Are You a Good Samaritan? Find Out Whether Bystanders Stop to Assist a Stranger in Need," ABC News, March 11, 2008, http://abcnews.go.com/print?id=4420829.
4. Donald Miller, *A Million Miles in a Thousand Years: What I Learned While Editing My Life* (Nashville: Thomas Nelson, 2009), 108.
5. Novogratz, *The Blue Sweater*, 18.
6. "Quotation Details: Quotation #35592," The Quotation Page, 2010, http://www.quotationspage.com/quote/35592.html.
7. Yamamori, Dageforde, and Bruner, eds., *The Hope Factor*, 228.
8. David Platt, *Radical: Taking Back Your Faith from the American Dream* (Colorado Springs: Multnomah Books, 2010), 19–20.
9. "OMF International: Annual Report 2008," OMF International, 2008, www.omf.org/content/download/13805/112218/file/Annual.
10. "Women's Quest: Fitness Retreats," Women's Quest, accessed on July 1, 2011, http://www.womensquest.com/documents/drive.pdf, 1.
11. Gary Haugen, *Just Courage: God's Great Expedition for the Restless Christian* (Downers Grove: InterVarsity Press, 2008), 124–125.
12. Vernon Brewer, "Risk it All," August 7, 2011, Thomas Road Baptist Church, Lynchburg, VA, http://trbclive.com/sermons.php?url=/20110807_11AM.html.
13. Miller, *A Million Miles in a Thousand Years*, 59.

Chapter 10 Let's Roll

1. "Elie Wiesel—Nobel Lecture: Hope, Despair, and Memory," NobelPrize.org, 1986, http://nobelprize.org/nobel_prizes/peace/laureates/1986/wiesel-lecture.html.

2. "Clinton: 'Justice Has Been Served,'" CNN Political Ticker, May 2, 2011, http://politicalticker.blogs.cnn.com/2011/05/02/clinton-justice-has-been-served/.

3. Lisa Beamer, *Let's Roll: Ordinary People, Extraordinary Courage* (Wheaton: Tyndale, 2002), 214.

4. Bob Minzesheimer, "Lisa Beamer: Mother First, Author Second," *USA Today*, August 19, 2002, http://www.usatoday.com/life/2002-08-18-beamer_x.htm.

5. "Lisa Beamer's Strength: Her Husband's Words Became a Rallying Cry for the Nation," *Dateline NBC*, August 20, 2002, http://www.msnbc.msn.com/id/3080111/ns/dateline_nbc-newsmakers/t/lisa-beamers-strength/.

6. Keller, *Generous Justice*, 15–16.

7. Mike and Danae Yankoski, *Zealous Love: A Practical Guide to Social Justice* (Grand Rapids: Zondervan, 2009), 51.

8. Richard Stearns, *The Hole in Our Gospel: What Does God Expect of Us? The Answer That Changed My Life and Might Just Change the World* (Nashville: Thomas Nelson, 2009), vi.

9. Keller, *Generous Justice*, 4.

10. Ibid., 9.

11. "The World Factbook: Rwanda," Central Intelligence Agency, June 14, 2011, https://www.cia.gov/library/publications/the-world-factbook/geos/rw.html.

12. "HIV/AIDS," TakingITGlobal, 2011, http://issues.tigweb.org/hiv.

13. "Rwanda: How the genocide happened," BBC, May 17, 2011, http://news.bbc.co.uk/1/hi/world/africa/1288230.stm.

14. "Rwanda: Facts and Figures," UNICEF, October, 2010, http://www.unicef.org/infobycountry/23867_20292.html.

15. Wendy Whitworth, *We Survived: Genocide in Rwanda* (Nottinghamshire, UK: Quill Press, 2006), 9.

16. Ibid.

17. Ibid., 11.

18. Ibid.

19. "Rwanda: Facts and Figures," UNICEF.

20. "Children's Memorial," Kigali Memorial Centre, Kigali, Rwanda, May 2007.

21. Barker, *Make Poverty Personal*, 22.

22. "Children's Memorial."

23. "Rwanda: Facts and Figures," UNICEF.

24. Lyons, *The Next Christians*, 47.

25. Gary Haugen, *Good News about Injustice: A Witness of Courage in a Hurting World*, 2nd ed. (Downers Grove: InterVarsity Press, 2009), 115.

26. "Famous Quotes about Children," Compassion, accessed January 2, 2012, http://www.compassion.com/child-advocacy/find-your-voice/famous-quotes/default.htm.

27. Haugen, 116.

28. Yamamori, Dageforde, and Bruner, eds., *The Hope Factor*, 264.

29. Ibid.

30. Palmer, *Divine Nobodies*, 146.

Chapter 11 Outraged, Loud, and Bold

1. Switchfoot, "This Is Your Life," *The Beautiful Letdown*, © 2003 Meadowgreen Music Company (ASCAP), Sugar Pete Songs (ASCAP) (admin. at EMICMG Publishing.com). All rights reserved. Used by permission.

2. "Gondola," Less Talk More Action commercial series, Royal Bank of Scotland, available online http://www.youtube.com/watch?v=byYQtv8NXGQ.

3. "Brad Pitt Quotes," Good Reads, 2011, http://www.goodreads.com/quotes/show/62174.

4. Lucado, *Outlive Your Life*, 106.

5. Mark DeMoss, *The Little Red Book of Wisdom* (Nashville: Thomas Nelson, 2007), 1.

6. Ibid., 6.

7. Zadra and Yamada, *1: How Many People Does It Take to Make a Difference?*, 22.

8. "Kindness Quotes," Spread Kindness, accessed December 21, 2011, http://www.spreadkindness.org/tools/kindness-quotes.

9. Andy Andrews, *The Traveler's Gift: Seven Decisions that Determine Personal Success* (Nashville: Thomas Nelson, 2005), 181.

10. Novogratz, *The Blue Sweater*, 254.

11. Personal correspondence. Used by permission.

12. Bob Pierce, as quoted in Stearns, *The Hole in Our Gospel*, 9.

13. Shane Claiborne, *Becoming the Answer to Our Prayers* (Downers Grove, IL: InterVarsity Press, 2008), 117-118.

14. "Martin Luther King Jr.," The Quotations Page, accessed January 2, 2012, http://www.quotationspage.com/quotes/Martin_Luther_King_Jr.

15. "Microsoft's Bill Gates: Harvard Commencement Speech Transcript," Network World, June 8, 2007, http://www.networkworld.com/news/2007/060807-gates-commencement.html?page=4.

16. Tom Brokaw, as quoted in Robert Consalvo, "Commencement 2008: Faculty Remarks," Bennington, VT: Southern Vermont College, 2008, http://svc.edu/pr/commencement_2008/consalvo_speech.html.

17. *Amazing Grace*, DVD, directed by Michael Apted (2007; Los Angeles: 20th Century Fox Home Entertainment, 2007).

18. U2, "I'll Go Crazy If I Don't Go Crazy Tonight," *No Line on the Horizon*, Interscope Records, 2009.

Noel Brewer Yeatts is the vice president of World Help (world help.net), a faith-based humanitarian organization that serves the physical and spiritual needs of people in impoverished communities around the world. She also directs an initiative of World Help, cause*life* (causelife.org), a movement of people dedicated to providing the most essential need to human life—clean water. Her work has taken her around the world to document the gripping stories of those affected by HIV/AIDS, hunger, poverty, and disease. The coauthor of two books and a noted speaker, Yeatts challenges thousands across the nation at universities, churches, conferences, and special events. She lives in Virginia. For more information, visit noelyeatts.com.

The author's proceeds from this book
will benefit the global initiatives
of World Help.

World_Help_

Help for Today . . . Hope for Tomorrow

PREVENTABLE DISEASES, WAR, POVERTY, and SPIRITUAL DARKNESS are robbing millions around the world of true and lasting hope.

THAT'S WHY WORLD HELP EXISTS.

World Help is a faith-based humanitarian organization that serves the physical and spiritual needs of people in impoverished communities around the world.

Through humanitarian, medical, and education assistance; ensuring access to clean water; providing Bibles; and establishing churches, World Help sustainably transforms lives.

Visit **worldhelp.net** *today to get involved.*

causelife

The need is overwhelming, but the solution is simple:

WATER EQUALS LIFE!

EVERY DAY, NEARLY A BILLION PEOPLE ACROSS THE GLOBE LIVE WITHOUT ACCESS TO CLEAN, SAFE DRINKING WATER.

cause**life** is a movement of people dedicated to changing this reality.

By raising global awareness, involving passionate activists and volunteers, and implementing practical clean-water solutions, cause**life** provides clean, safe water that changes lives and transforms communities.

Join the movement today by visiting cause**life**.org

AWAKE

Doing a World of Good One Person at a Time

WHAT'S AVAILABLE ONLINE:

Videos for each chapter

Photo gallery of stories from the book

Initiatives and opportunities for you to
do a world of good

Join the *Awake* community and share
your story

WWW.AWAKEBOOK.ORG